C000021706

YOUNG, HOMELESS AND FORGOTTEN

Barry Stillerman

Grosvenor House
Publishing Limited

This book is published by
Grosvenor House Publishing Ltd
Link House
140 The Broadway, Tolworth, Surrey, KT6 7HT.
www.grosvenorhousepublishing.co.uk

A CIP record for this book
is available from the British Library

ISBN 978-1-83975-005-2

CONTENTS

PART I

THE ISSUES

'A fifth of young people are homeless – you just can't see them'.

Source: *The Guardian* and The London Assembly,
27th September 2017.

1

THE YOUTH HOMELESS CRISIS

Introduction

Like many, my first encounter with homeless people was engaging with rough sleepers on the streets of London. I just could not understand why there were so many homeless people in the capital of one of the richest countries in the world and, as I delved deeper, I started to examine the complex nature of homelessness.

Rough sleeping is a small proportion of the total homeless population. There are huge numbers of 'hidden homeless' who are out of sight and out of mind to most people. After 20 years, you never stop learning, but I now have a better understanding of the relevant issues and what can be done to change the current situation.

I became particularly concerned over the plight of vulnerable young people aged between 18 and 24 (as, up to 18, the state is responsible). Like older members of the public, these young people have a broad range of abilities, skills and issues but require support to overcome their individual problems. Many have identified their future goals and a career that they wish to pursue. They are often very resilient but are currently being prevented from moving forward and achieving independence.

So many of the homeless young people I have met have had an unfortunate start in life. You would not choose an abusive stepfather or to see your mother unable to provide for your basic needs. You may have fled a war zone and are trying to make a new life in unfamiliar surroundings. In my experience, most young, homeless people do not want a handout but rather an opportunity to lead what most of us would regard as a normal life.

As Nigel Ferndale reported in *The Times* article on 24th August 2019, "If you want something done, ask a 25-year-old", as youngsters are at their peak at this age. Our cognitive development continues into our mid-twenties, at which time, when our wiring connections are finally complete, we reach our creative and intellectual maturity.

There are many examples of great achievements from young people, such as Sir Paul McCartney, Mozart and Schubert. Einstein was that age when he discovered the theory of special relativity, while Magnus Carlsen became the world chess champion at 22. Many young people who suddenly find themselves homeless have the ability to rise above their current plight if they can be given the right support at this critical time.[1]

They are at a crossroads where one path can lead to a downward spiral of poverty, unemployment and possible issues with mental health, criminality and drug abuse, and the other can result in an enjoyable life as a valuable member of society. There is a short timeframe before their problems become long-term in nature.

In discussions with friends, I found that there was a general misperception of youth homelessness and a poor appreciation of the problems that these young people face. I also began to question the way that homelessness is handled in the UK.

So as to reduce paper throughout this book, I refer to homeless young people as 'HYP'. Also, while the cases in this book are

---

[1] Article 'If you want something done, ask a 25-year-old', Nigel Ferndale, *The Times,* 24th August 2019.

real, I have anonymised some people involved so as to protect their identity.

Background

My own background is in the service sector, and you may ask what this has to do with homelessness but stay with me for a few paragraphs and I hope that it will become clear.

I qualified as a chartered accountant and, as a partner at Stoy Hayward (now BDO), enjoyed advising clients on financial matters. I subsequently became the lead partner in the tax consultancy group and this gave me experience in running a division of the firm, with all that this entails.

One day, a client asked me to look at an investment proposal he had received. It quickly became apparent that the proposed investment was far too risky when compared to the mandate he had given the adviser and that the plan was structured to provide the investment salesman with high commission paid for by my client.

It struck me that our clients were open to abuse from the investment industry, which was rife with conflicts of interest, and that we could provide a much better service but would need to gain the right level of expertise. With backing from my partners, I was able to set up a service for clients that was designed to provide trustworthy, added value advice.

I set about analysing how various investments worked and, over time and with help of specialists from the investment world, was able to create investment products that outperformed many of my competitors by approaching the subject differently from the crowd.

To give you one example, before multi-manager funds became popular, I found that many of my clients used traditional stockbrokers who would buy shares in companies that were based in the UK, US, Europe and the Far East. I could not understand how one investment house could have the best managers in each of these geographical regions. I started to seek out the best fund managers for each sector and put them together in a fund that produced better risk-adjusted returns when compared to the more traditional managers and other multi-manager funds taking account of all charges.

Analysing the homeless sector

So, coming back to the homeless crisis, for more than a decade, I have been looking at how homeless people are being served in the UK. The more I looked into the problem, the more I found deficiencies in the system and started to examine better ways to provide the same service. I started to question whether there is any likelihood of matters improving to an extent where youth homelessness can be significantly reduced and not yoyo back up again.

I studied methods used by certain overseas charities that have successfully helped thousands of HYP achieve independence. I also met with numerous homeless charities in the UK, both large and small, as well as the specialists that provide support services. I helped to create homes that are helping young people transition from homelessness to a fully independent life and then started to look at the bigger picture: the funding requirements and how this country could tackle the problem on a long-term basis.

I readily admit that this book looks at possible solutions rather than cures and that homelessness often arises from deep-seated social problems. I also understand why people tend to support causes close to home.

Statistically, more families will be affected by cancer than homelessness, so I absolutely understand why someone would want to devote their resources to medical research or other charitable projects.

I have come across many people who want to do something for the homeless but do not know how, or what to do; ranging from those who have little money but time to help, up to the ultra-high net worth who are in a position to make a huge difference. Everyone can play a part, if communities work together to improve the lives of others.

A national disgrace

On 22nd November 2018, BBC News reported that 320,000 people had been recorded as homeless in Britain, based upon analysis from the housing charity Shelter. It was a rise of 13,000 (4%) on the previous year's figures and equivalent to 36 new people becoming homeless every day. This accounts for about one in every 200 Britons.

The data was compiled after collating official figures for those living in temporary accommodation, sleeping rough and the number of hostel places taken up, reducing them to compensate for double counting. The charity commented that its figures are likely to be a conservative estimate, as they do not include people unknown to the authorities or experiencing other types of homelessness not included in the figures. For example, the hidden homeless and sofa surfers, by their very nature, are difficult to find.

London had the highest rate, but it was growing fast in the Midlands, Yorkshire and the Humber and north-west England. The government reported that it is investing £1.2 billion in tackling homelessness, but still the numbers rise. Newham had the highest homeless ratio in London – one in 25.

It should also be borne in mind that many rough sleepers, particularly women, will be hidden from view to protect their safety and so may not be counted. In addition, the headcount by local authorities takes place on a single autumn night and the results can be influenced by the weather, where people sleep and the availability of facilities such as night shelters.

There are various other reports on the size of the homeless population. The June 2018 report 'Assessing the costs and benefits of Crisis' plan to end homelessness' produced by Pricewater-houseCoopers for Crisis projected the costs and benefits of ending homelessness in the UK. It was based upon 246,000 households that will need support in 2018 (rising to nearly 436,000 by 2041, with unchanged policies).

To link households to individual people, the August 2017 report by Professor Glen Bramley for Crisis referred to 160,000 core homeless households. The 2017 households comprised 57,000 family households (containing 82,000 adults and 50,000 children – 132,000 individuals) together with 103,000 single people. This makes a total of 235,000 people from 160,000 households – a ratio of approximately 1.5 people to a core homeless household.

However, again, these numbers are bad enough but they excluded the wider homeless, which includes the HYP staying with friends or relatives because they are unable to find accommodation, or have just been evicted, discharged from prison, hospital or other temporary accommodation, without anywhere to stay. It also includes those who have received a notice to quit and are unable to afford rent or a deposit, or have been asked to leave by friends or relatives and are in temporary accommodation.

We can see that the number of homeless people is unacceptable, whichever report you read. We will consider the current level of youth homelessness later in this book but clearly the numbers are large enough to lead to the conclusion that urgent and effective action is required, rather than bland statements of intent.

Coming back to rough sleepers, an annual headcount of the number of people sleeping on the streets indicated that, in 2018, rough sleepers fell by 2% in the UK (although rough sleeping in the capital rose by 13%). It led James Brokenshire, the communities secretary, to announce that this was a step in the right direction. However, it was quickly pointed out that although the figures are classed as official statistics, they are widely held to underestimate the actual number of people sleeping rough. Also, as Crisis pointed out, rough sleeping had increased by 165% since records began in 2010.

So what most people see is just the tip of the iceberg, as rough sleeping is less than 10% of the total homeless numbers. Even beyond homeless numbers, many people are only just coping and it would not take much for them to fall over the edge.

In the past, you could expect to find a job and be there for life. Now it is extremely rare to find someone who has worked in one job for several decades. New technology is changing the face of the workplace and the high street. Zero hours contracts may be acceptable for those who are confident that their services are in demand but can be really problematic for many struggling to pay their monthly bills. The employment sector must react to these changes.

The purpose of this book

The purpose of this book is to:

- examine the current, false perception of youth homelessness;
- provide a better understanding of the required support needs of HYP;
- identify deficiencies in the current provisions of housing and support;
- explore ways in which housing and support can be improved;
- consider the roles of the state, charity sector, private sector and the public;
- examine the creation of a caring home model to transition HYP to an independent life;
- consider the funding and resourcing to significantly reduce youth homelessness;
- consider what we can all do to assist in the process.

Part I of this book seeks to provide readers with an understanding of the issues relating to youth homelessness. It describes what it is like for a young person to suddenly face homelessness. We consider the size of the problem and why the government's statistics do not cover the homeless population. We examine the current perception of youth homelessness and why it is often way off the mark and its support needs.

The various reasons for homelessness are outlined and I have used real life cases in this book so that you can see how many young people are trying to cope with the problems that they face. It will become clear that a joined-up approach is needed. I have also taken advantage of the extensive research that has already been produced, both in the UK and abroad.

Getting young people off the streets may make the problem seem to disappear but to move a young person to an independent life will require all the issues that gave rise to their situation to be addressed, as temporary housing can often extend the chaotic nature of their plight.

In Part II, we take stock and consider the position in the UK and the deficiencies in the provision of support for young people in crisis. Unfortunately, even in this highly technological age, there are no accurate statistics on the size of the problem, especially as many young people are part of the homeless population that is hidden from view. This needs to be addressed so that we can monitor and keep appraised of the success or otherwise of any action taken to tackle youth homelessness.

HYP can be found in a wide variety of accommodation, much of which is not appropriate if that young person is struggling to complete studies that may have been disrupted or find a job. The potential for better identifying young people in crisis is an important part of dealing with a problem before it becomes too difficult to handle.

Part III looks at the various parties involved in helping to tackle youth homelessness. There are a wide range of homeless charities, including those that were set up specifically to help HYP. The types of service differ and, in some cases, a number of charities are used to bring together all the services required for a particular case. Some charities have sought to provide many of the services in-house, while others outsource what cannot be provided.

The role of the state is examined, as this would be the natural place to start and generally the institution that gets the blame for the problems in society. However, how practical is it to rely on the state taking account of the demands from its various ministries? On the other hand, should the state be let off the hook, if others pick up the tab? We consider a practical approach that can bridge the gap. Where does the private sector fit in? What role should wealthy benefactors play? We will look at a number of ways that members of the public can have an important role to play.

The final part of this book examines different approaches and the planning of one home using a fully integrated approach to service provision that can be replicated around the UK. We consider which resources are required to tackle youth homelessness, in terms of money and people, and where these may be found. It calls for a way forward that involves all members of society who have an interest in saving young people in crisis and helping them to help themselves to achieve a fully independent life at this critical time. What is required is a lasting approach, so that youth homelessness does not merely get hidden from view or neglected due to the state of the economy at any point in time.

As I live in London and understand the youth homeless scene better here than in other parts of the country, some of the references are a little London-centric, but most of the issues raised in this book apply across the UK, to a greater or lesser extent.

A business-like approach

In my professional and business life, running and advising companies, often my starting point was to create a business plan and then follow through its implementation while monitoring performance against budget.

I have read numerous UK and international research papers but could not find a detailed strategic plan for the wider homeless situation that set out all the problems that need to be overcome, identified the key players and explained how the necessary funds would be made available and the properties found so that the current unacceptable levels of homelessness will fall both significantly and permanently.

As I could not identify a cohesive strategy to reduce youth homelessness, I decided to examine the current position in more depth and discuss the various issues arising with specialists at various homeless charities that help young people on a daily basis and are experts in their field.

Towards the end of this book, we examine the scale of the task, with costs and resources broken down so that individual communities or small groups can be part of the solution.

Action must be taken now and the success of individual projects can lead to a more comprehensive, nationwide, fully costed plan being put in place. Broad goals are one thing but a detailed plan that is monitored against performance and publicised should give rise to greater trust in the process.

2

PERCEPTION AND REALITY

The projected image

There was no word for 'homeless' in the Japanese language until after World War II, when their government made provisions, calling such people *Furou* or *Runpen*; roughly translated as vagrant or loafer. More recently, the Japanese government has used the term, 'persons of no fixed abode' as the complexities of homelessness became clearer, showing a change of approach.[2]

The Framework Institute study conducted across the UK during 2017 and 2018 looked at how the general public understands and responds to the way that homelessness is framed. The study revealed a strong, and factually incorrect, view among the public that homeless people are primarily rough sleeping older white men, and that their homelessness is caused by bad life choices and addictions.[3]

The public also equate homelessness with people living on the streets in the absence of a roof over their head. This is problematic not only because it misrepresents the full range of homelessness but also because it blocks an understanding of other forms.

---

[2] 'A comparative study of homelessness in the UK and Japan', Yoshihiro Okamoto, *Journal of Social Issues,* Vol 63, No 3 ,2007 pp. 525-542.
[3] Report 'Everybody in: How to end homelessness in Great Britain', Crisis and Frameworks reporting for Crisis, 2018.

Homelessness is understood as a state completely outside of, and alien to, normal human existence.

Jules de Barsham grew up in a loving, supportive home with a degree-level education. He enjoyed a successful career, took early retirement in his 50s, but found himself to be homeless after his relationship imploded. He had always had an affluent lifestyle. By 24 he was a successful advertising copywriter and had bought his first home. He admits that he would harangue a rough sleeper 'to get a job', never imagining how tenuous his own situation would one day become. The concept of ever losing his home or job was unthinkable.

Jules moved into the entertainment industry and, at 50, he took early retirement and finally started a family with his new partner. However, after the relationship broke down in a very acrimonious manner, he left his home, partner and young son. This gradually led to rough sleeping and three years of homelessness. He has finally found a flat with a friend from the night shelter and is rebuilding his life. Jules regards himself as living proof that becoming homeless can happen to anyone.[4]

'The Salt Path' is the uplifting true story of a couple who lost everything and embarked on a journey of salvation across the windswept South West coastline. It has been a *Sunday Times* bestseller and was shortlisted for the 2018 Costa Biography Award and The Wainwright Prize. Written by Raynor Winn and published by Penguin UK, it tells how the author reacted to losing her home and business and received news that her husband had a terminal illness; all within a week. Here are two people who had led a normal life and brought up two children but suddenly found themselves to be homeless. During their travels they met many people along the coastal path but the book also refers to an

---

[4] Article 'How it feels to... lose it all and end up living on the streets', Jules de Barsham, *The Sunday Times Magazine*, 13th October 2019.

occasion when a family recoiled from them when learning that they were homeless.

A prototype of HYP is someone who has been kicked out by the family and is assumed to be living on the streets because of some dysfunction in the family home. This activates individualistic thinking about families and makes it difficult to see any structural reasons why young people might be homeless.

'A fifth of young people are homeless – you just can't see them'

I read this article by Paul Noblet for *The Guardian* and thought that the headline was worth repeating. It is estimated that there are 13 times more hidden homeless people in London than those who are sleeping rough and that 225,000 young people have stayed in an unsafe place because they have nowhere to call home.[5] An added problem with this group is that some people may feel that if they have a roof over their head and there are support services available, they are a less urgent problem.

The inability for HYP to move forward due to the chaotic situation that they find themselves in is not well understood. Stories about how people lapse into homelessness (for example through drug and alcohol addiction) raise unproductive questions about whether this person (or any homeless person) is worthy of help from society. While substance abuse is not uncommon, the main reason for youth homelessness is relationship breakdown.

There are various support needs required by HYP, covering issues such as mental health, substance abuse, poverty and criminality – in some cases a resort to petty crime has been a reflection of the need for food or a room at a hostel to get off the streets rather than a disrespect for property. Members of the public can be

---

[5]   Article 'A fifth of young people are homeless – you just can't see them', Paul Noblet, *The Guardian* and The London Assembly, 27th September 2017.

reticent to speak to a homeless person, let property to people on benefits or support homeless charities.

I met one man in his 20s who, having become a young parent himself, replicated the lifestyle of his mother, leading to homelessness, drug addiction and a life of theft and violence. I am not accepting any of this behaviour but I could see that he had never had a decent role model, nor anyone who believed in him or felt that he could change for the better. He is not yet ready to start the process of getting clean, trying to find employment and become financially independent. He does not want to live off benefits but is running up ever increasing debts. Unfortunately, there are many similar cases and too few trained staff who have the time and expertise to start the healing process.

While some people have become homeless due to a development of these issues prior to homelessness, others have developed issues of this kind *because of* homelessness. The key is to provide the right level of support at an early stage of homelessness so that these problems do not develop or worsen.

Many members of the public assume that individual acts of charity towards people in crisis are effective and sufficient in addressing homelessness. The obvious drawback is that if one-off charitable acts are seen as sufficient, then the appetite for tackling structural causes or advocating prevention measures can be seriously inhibited.

Fake begging

Another issue that has come into the public eye is the case of fake beggars on the streets. The media has run articles and TV programmes that have highlighted this problem. While there are cases of fake begging (and it tends to be more prevalent among the general population than the youth) it is generally relatively small in relation to the number of HYP.

It is important to get this problem into perspective. What is not known is how many 'fake homeless' people there are in Britain.

However, Merseyside Police have said that only 8% of people arrested for begging between 2015 and 2018 had accommodation.[6]

Vigilante campaigns to drive fake homeless people off the street were condemned by police and local authorities. Police said that the dangerous practice of 'outing' people as professional criminals based on often unverified information fails to acknowledge the very complex vulnerabilities and chaotic lives of those concerned.[7]

Any concern about fake begging should not be allowed to deflect attention from the true level of youth homelessness in the UK. Homeless charities have felt that people are now demonising the true homeless people who already face a lack of trust and abuse from the public. It also makes it important that donations are channelled in the right direction.

Changing perception

Considerable work is needed to explain the causes of homelessness such that people can see the potential power of intervening early or pre-emptively, and imagine ways of doing so, to avoid problems and create better outcomes. Research has also shown that a further challenge is the issue of fatalism, or the idea that the public see homelessness as inevitable and unsolvable.

There was a great deal of publicity on homelessness in the lead-up to Christmas 2018 and it will be interesting to see what effect this may have had when the next homeless research report is published. It is regrettable that, to date, the homeless sector has not always coordinated its communication efforts and that charities are often competing for media coverage or fundraising attention.

---

[6] Documentary 'Fake Homeless: Who's Begging on the Streets?', presenter Ellie Flynn, BBC Three, 8th January 2019.
[7] Article 'Vigilante campaign to drive "fake homeless people" off the streets condemned by police and local authority', May Bulman, *The Independent*, 27th February 2018.

However, the public's concerns have changed in recent years. A poll issued in early January 2019 showed that the third most important issues facing Britain were poverty and inequality; not unexpectedly behind Brexit and the NHS. This is despite the record numbers in work, although this can partly be explained by weak pay growth in recent years. The Joseph Rowntree Foundation says that 4 million workers are living in poverty and two-thirds of the 4.1 million children living in poverty are in working households.[8]

The perception of charitable giving is a subject of concern to those who seek to donate to large projects. Bill Gates, one of the largest charitable benefactors, has been infuriated by the headlines from Africa being all about either pitiful orphans with huge eyes or corrupt aid projects. *"The world operates in stories and, irritatingly, stories of one life saved or a tiny amount of money being spent corruptly are way better than millions of people saved. It's way more evocative. If I jumped in a river and grabbed a child it would be taken more seriously than the millions of lives we saved."* He is also impatient with the cynicism that surrounds charitable giving in Britain. *"You are the most generous with your Red Nose Day and Comic Relief, but you also criticise aid in a way that no other country does. It's bizarre."*[9]

Mixed messages

This approach to charitable giving was part of the row that erupted when Labour MP David Lammy raised the subject of the 'white saviour complex'. It is difficult to assess its effect in financial terms but in 2019, Comic Relief suffered an £8 million fall in funds raised by its Red Nose Day appeal, down from £71.3 million in 2018 to £63 million in 2019, and well below the record

---

[8] Article 'Record Numbers in work, so why is poverty going up?', David Smith, *The Sunday Times*, 13th January 2019, Ipsos Mori poll.
[9] Article 'How does the world's second richest man relax?', Alice Thompson, *The Times*, 16th March 2019.

£108 million raised in 2011. Even so, these are huge amounts raised by the British public.[10]

Documentaries on homelessness can make for interesting viewing but often do not help the youth homelessness cause. Channel 4 aired '60 days on the streets' in March 2019, showing former soldier Ed Stafford's experiences of spending winter months sleeping rough in London, Manchester and Glasgow. It included encounters with many middle-aged people who had been homeless for some years, and you would have struggled to envisage how they could be brought back into the wider community.

Some had no intention of changing their lifestyle, while others showed how you could make decent money begging. Many used the money to buy drugs, even though it appeared, at first, that the money was to be used to find shelter. There were even beggars who had a home, even though they had formerly been homeless. On some occasions, well intended members of the public bought food for those on the street but this resulted in some having more than they needed that day. I felt, after the first two episodes, that most people would be less encouraged to help, considering the plight of the homeless people as self-inflicted.

The last of the three episodes showed the progress made in Scotland in reducing rough sleeping. It reported that only 30 people were sleeping rough in Glasgow out of a population of around 600,000; a significantly lower ratio than in London.

The comparatively better position in Glasgow appeared to be due to progressive laws and money spent on providing housing stock. It also showed the excellent work from volunteers at winter shelters and street food provisions. However, it also recognised that the problem of homelessness was moving from rough sleeping to hidden homelessness and that a more permanent solution was

---

[10] Article 'No laughing matter – Comic Relief down £8m after "white saviour" row', Nicholas Hellen, *The Sunday Times*, 17th March 2019.

needed to enable these people to have a chance of getting back into society.

One homeless person interviewed recognised that his plight was due to bad life choices. However, there appeared to be a lack of counselling to identify the problems behind substance abuse and there did not appear to be a way forward that would encourage a life without alcohol or drugs. Many middle-aged people who had been homeless for some time started on a downward path due to trauma early in their life and were finding it hard to see a way forward, having become used to a life of homelessness.

The programme was helpful in highlighting a misuse of people's good intentions and does reinforce the better approach of donating to homeless charities that understand the day to day issues. However, I felt that anyone watching the programme would wonder why it is worth helping when they may be being taken for a ride.

'Death on the Streets' was the lead article of *The Times* issue of 2nd October 2019. It reported that, every day, on average, two rough sleepers in England and Wales were dying; the highest annual rise since figures began to be kept – nearly half from a drug overdose. Greg Hurst's article in the same edition, 'Rough sleeper deaths hit record high', reported 726 deaths in 2018, of whom most were men with an average age of 45.[11]

There a number of messages that can be taken. In the first place, the rise in deaths from homelessness is shocking. However, again, it focuses on what the public can see – rough sleeping but not the hidden homeless. The issue of death from drug overdose leads some to shy away from supporting homeless causes. However, severely shortened life expectancy shows what can happen to HYP

---

[11] Articles 'Death on the Streets', *The Times*, and 'Rough sleeper deaths hit record high', Greg Hurst, *The Times*, 2nd October 2019.

if they are not supported at an early stage and go on to remain homeless over the long-term.

Many HYP are at the start of the homeless cycle; a critical time when they could either work towards an independent life or join those who are currently regarded as 'institutionally' homeless. These young people firstly need permanent accommodation (or at least temporary accommodation for a short period of time, until a more permanent housing solution is found).

The charities that need additional funding are those that can assess HYP, work with them over a period of time, understand their needs and provide tailored support for those who want to make a go of their lives.

Health issues

Over the past two decades, much research has been dedicated to exploring the relationship between health and homelessness. In one study, 85% of people experiencing homelessness reported having a chronic health condition. These problems included:

- Mortality and survival rates;
- Unintentional injuries (bruises, cuts, burns);
- Musculoskeletal disorders and chronic pain;
- Hunger and nutrition;
- Skin and foot problems;
- Infectious diseases;
- Dental problems;
- Respiratory illness;
- Chronic diseases and disorders;
- Sexual and reproductive care;
- Mental health issues.[12]

---

[12] Report 'What are the top ten health issues for homeless people?', Emma Woolley, Research Assistant, Canadian Observatory on Homelessness/Homeless Hub, York University, 6th February 2015.

It is a sobering thought that, in 2011, the BBC reported that, based on research for Crisis, the average homeless person had a life expectancy of 47, compared with 77 for the rest of the population.

What it is it like to be homeless in the UK

Ian Williams explained what it is like to be homeless on 30th November 2016, as shown on the web. He wrote, *"I was homeless in the UK when I was 19 and your experience depends entirely on your circumstances. I was very lucky that a certain series of events occurred when they did, which made my time a lot easier, but it was still harder than anyone who has not experienced it could possibly imagine.*

I was made homeless by an unscrupulous landlord who decided he was selling the house. He did not tell me this at the time it was happening. The first I heard of it was when I was given 24 hours' notice (completely illegal) to vacate the house. This guy was not someone you said no to, or argued with, so I had no choice.

I went to a local homeless shelter, but they had no room as it was winter and the homeless population had got there first. Luckily for me, there was a hospital literally right next door to the shelter and it was being completely refurbished over the Christmas period.

I didn't dare go inside as there were workmen coming and going all times of the day and night and I didn't want to get thrown out. Instead, I found an outbuilding (more of a glorified brick shed) at the rear of the hospital which the builders were throwing all their cardboard packaging into, ready to be recycled at the end of the renovation. It was completely full to overflowing with boxes and sheet cardboard.

This shed was completely watertight so I literally burrowed through the boxes into the far corner, furthest from the door.

I arranged a few boxes to hide my tunnel and unless you knew exactly where to look, it was completely invisible. I made a little den using a very large cardboard box and made a bed with several layers of hospital bedsheets taken from a skip the builders couldn't see in the evenings once it started to get dark.

I also had my own sleeping bag with the meagre belongings I was able to take with me when I was forced from my home. It was horrible, but it was warm and dry. I was much more fortunate than many other homeless people I knew.

Let me tell you something. Being homeless is both extremely boring and psychological torture from start to finish. This is something you can never experience unless you actually become homeless in real life. I understand why many take to drugs or alcohol to numb themselves. Many people attend 'sleep-outs' to experience homelessness, but trust me, it is not the same at all, even if those people experience sleeping rough. As far as I am concerned, all those people are doing is camping poorly.

To be homeless is to have no hope. You have nothing, you have no hope of getting anything. People abuse you all day and scream at you to just a get a job. It's not that simple. I'm highly educated, but not a single one of you reading this would give me a job for two very good and valid reasons. First, a job requires an address, which you don't have. Second, who in their right mind would employ someone who has not been able to wash or shower for a few weeks? No one. I know that for a fact as I tried, multiple times. I was dirty, my clothes were dirty and I smelled really bad. Quite frankly, I was a health hazard and employers would not have been allowed to give me a job in that state, even if they wanted too.

You have no idea when, or even if, your situation will ever improve so you have no option than to resign yourself to it, quickly. This is the psychological torture. You cannot claim benefits without a physical address so I had no money except the few remaining pounds in my bank account, but they went within the first two weeks.

There is help available, but not if you were like me. I was 'normal'. I was not an alcoholic. I was not a drug user. I was male, therefore neither pregnant nor classed as vulnerable. I was not on any form of medication and not mentally ill. I do not have a learning disability and I had never been in prison. If you were any of those things, there is immediate help available. And by immediate, I mean you get help, right there and then. The council was required to give you immediate temporary accommodation. I was a normal single male so not entitled to anything. Sadly, that's still the case with many local authorities all over the UK today.

It is cold, it is wet and it is lonely. There might be loads of you in a group looking out for each other, but at the end of the day, it's each man for himself and everyone knows that. Homelessness is not something you can ever adequately prepare yourself for, nor is it ever something you can experience, unless you are actually experiencing it for real."[13]

While there are a number of different categories of homeless people who are in urgent need of help, in particular homeless families with young children, I feel that if we can find a way to help the vulnerable young people to move from homelessness to a fully independent life, not only do you take a large group away from danger but there is a good chance that these people will become valuable members of society, making a positive contribution to this country.

Like in any age group, there are those who are more forward looking and some who will need serious guidance if they are to progress, but only if we can find a way to unlock their potential.

---

[13] Web response, 'What does it feel like to be homeless?' by Ian Williams, 30th November 2016.

So, having established that we want to seriously reduce youth homelessness, we need to drill down further.

Popularity

You Gov produce a list of UK charities by popularity and you have to go a long way down the list to find any that help the homeless. I list below the top 10 with their percentage rating:

- St John Ambulance (86%);
- Macmillan Cancer Support (86%);
- Great Ormond Street Hospital (84%);
- Cancer Research UK (84%);
- Marie Curie (83%);
- British Heart Foundation (82%);
- Guide Dogs (81%);
- RNLI Lifeboats (80%);
- Alzheimer's Research UK (79%);
- Royal British Legion (78%).

The charities in the top 50 that had some association with the homeless were:

- Samaritans (78%) – 11th;
- British Red Cross (77%) – 14th;
- Help for Heroes (74%) – 19th;
- NSPCC (74%) – 20th;
- BBC Children in Need (71%) – 22nd;
- Barnardo's (70%) – 24th;
- Salvation Army (68%) – 28th;
- Save the Children (67%) – 30th;
- Comic Relief (63%) – 35th;
- Shelter (63%) – 37th;
- Prince's Trust and Prince of Wales Trust (62% and 60%) 39th and 41st respectively.[14]

---

[14] List of 'The most popular charities & organisations in the UK', You Gov.

It is only really Shelter that I would regard as a traditional homeless charity and its clients tend to be over 25 years of age. While recognising the popularity of many UK charities it also highlights the difficulty of UK youth homeless charities being heard.

Fundraising

Perhaps more importantly, homeless charities did not feature too highly when it came to fundraising. The Charity Financials Annual Report April 2019 listed the top 100 fundraising charities 2017/18, showing their fundraising income and total income. The top 10 charities in terms of funds (with their total income in brackets) raised were:

- Cancer Research £433m (£634m);
- British Heart Foundation £295m (£328m);
- Sightsavers International £291m (£321m);
- MacMillan Cancer Support £229m (£252m);
- Oxfam GB £200m (£427m);
- Royal National Lifeboat Institution £184m (£202m);
- British Red Cross Society £159m (£284m);
- Salvation Army £152m (£231m);
- Royal Society for the Prevention of Cruelty to Animals £118m (£140m);
- Save the Children £109m (£406m).

Those charities in the top 50 that had some association with the homeless were:

- NSPCC 12th £102m (£118m);
- Comic Relief 23rd £73m (£104m);
- BBC Children in Need 26th £62m (£67);
- Christian Aid 30th £54m (117m);
- Prince's Trust 37th £47m (72m);
- Shelter 39th (45m 67m);
- Barnardo's 41st £40m (304m);

Again, it is only Shelter that I would regard as a charity that is wholly focused on homelessness, but mainly for those over the age of 25.

Reputational issues

With so many problems faced by society, youth homelessness is fighting to be heard. Each Christmas, Crisis at Christmas gets good coverage and many people volunteer to help. In 2018, the media picked up the issue of homelessness in the UK but there is still a misunderstanding surrounding the numbers involved and the problems related to hidden homelessness.

A recent study by the Charities Aid Foundation found that the proportion of Britons who donate to charity or sponsor someone who is fundraising has fallen, for the third year in a row. While the drop is relatively small, the report suggests that charities are struggling to recover from a series of scandals.

Oxfam is the latest charity to damage the sector's reputation, having covered up allegations of staff sexually exploiting victims of the 2010 earthquake in Haiti. Stories of harassment at Save the Children and a 'toxic culture' at Amnesty International have made matters worse. The public has been put off by some charities' aggressive approach to fundraising.

Fewer than half thought that charities were trustworthy. This is an impediment to charitable giving that must be overcome if we are to make the kind of progress needed to create a fairer society. Baroness Stowell of Beeston has been appointed to chair the Charity Commission and has put restoring faith at the centre of her mission, while tighter regulation is being put in place.

Homeless charities are competing with other charitable causes for money and attention. I am sure that the homeless charities are doing everything they can to publicise the issues but perhaps a different approach would help, taking account of the misperceptions and scandals.

The message

It is amazing what can be achieved by one person thinking outside the box. This was highlighted recently by Greta Thunberg. The 16-year-old Swedish student became so concerned with climate change that she started skipping school every Friday to campaign for change. From August 2018, she started a weekly protest outside the Swedish Parliament building. This led to the schools' climate strikes that became an international campaign. She addressed the European Parliament, the World Economic Forum in Davos and government ministers in the UK and even met the Pope. She tapped into a real concern that many people felt, supported by scientific evidence of the changes taking place and the action needed to reverse the trend.

It is too early to tell whether the greater awareness of the problem will give rise to the kind of worldwide action that will reverse the current direction of global warming but the publicity at the time was extraordinary.

The challenge for the homeless sector is to provide a greater awareness of the problems and the action needed to permanently reduce the number of young people in crisis. It also needs to win back the trust of donors. In the case of ultra-high net worth donors, this can be achieved by identifying the scale of the problem, the opportunities to make a real difference and ensuring openness when it comes to reviewing finances and operational practices so that more people can be an important part of the solution.

3

THE SCALE OF THE PROBLEM

Initial estimates

While urgent action is now needed to permanently reduce youth homelessness, a national plan requires accurate data on the numbers involved so as to consider the resources required to tackle the problem and work towards updating those estimates into more accurate information.

As there were 236,000 households in the UK in 2018 needing support, with an average household size of 1.5 people, this would equate to over 350,000 people in 2018.[15] So, if there were 350,000 core homeless people, the total would be much larger when you take account of the hidden homeless.

Shelter has, more recently, estimated that at least 320,000 people are homeless in Britain. This figure was reached by combining government homelessness and rough sleeping statistics at July 2018 with data on homeless hostel bed spaces and social services provision of temporary accommodation for families in crisis. This number is also likely to be an under-estimate, as there will be some people in the hidden homeless category.

---

[15]   Summary report, 'Homelessness projections: core homelessness in Great Britain', Professor Glen Bramley for Crisis, August 2017.

As we shall see, one of the top reasons for a young person to be homeless is family breakdown or rejection. Therefore these recorded numbers are not a true reflection of the total number of homeless people in the UK. In 2018, it was reported that there has been a rise of 60% of families and individuals in temporary accommodation since 2012 and a huge rise in rough sleeping since 2010.

The bulk of those affected, 295,000, are in forms of temporary accommodation after being accepted as homeless by their local authority.[16] As we considered, when examining the perception of homelessness, while the public often identify rough sleeping with homelessness, far more are homeless but not necessarily on the streets. It is projected that the number of homeless people in Britain will reach 575,000 by 2041 and that those sleeping rough will more than quadruple over the same period.[17]

The forecast comes as the number of homeless households has jumped by a third in the past five years. The majority of those affected are 'sofa surfers', with the biggest rise coming from those placed by a local authority in unsuitable accommodation, such as bed and breakfasts, with the total expected to rise sharply. We are therefore dealing with large numbers of homeless people and an unreliable system that misses many who are hidden when making an attempt to quantify the population.

The problem with statistics like these is that it is difficult to appreciate the full extent of the problem. Joseph Stalin understood this concept well. During his rule, it is estimated that 20 million people were sent to labour camps where nearly half died – as he said at the time, *"A single death is a tragedy, a million deaths is a statistic."*

To try to put the numbers into some form of context, our national football stadium at Wembley has a maximum capacity of 90,000.

---

[16] Article 'At least 320,000 homeless people in Britain, says Shelter', Patrick Butler, *The Guardian*, 22nd November 2018.
[17] Report 'Number of homeless in Britain expected to double by 2041, Crisis warns', Sarah Marsh, 10th August 2017.

Just imagine the entire stadium full of homeless people, and then multiply that number by say four or five, and you get nearer to the homeless population in the UK.

Just about managing

A new term has been coined by politicians – the JAMs, those just about managing. Of course, it may take very little to tip the JAMs into homelessness and for the homeless crisis to worsen. JAM households have at least one person in work but are half as likely to have a degree as the rest of the population.

The Resolution Foundation says that they are not always 'low-income' households. Those making as much as £50,000 a year could be included, if they have several children to feed and clothe. Most of their income comes from work, but they are often topped up by welfare support. In fact, JAMs account for two-thirds of all families with children receiving tax credits and more than two-thirds have less than a month's savings to fall back upon.

The Trussell Trust is the largest food bank network in the UK and it handed out 1.2 million food parcels in 2016/17 as compared to 41,000 in 2009/10. As some people use food parcels more than once (on average twice a year) it estimates that 590,000 different people were using its services. In the year to March 2019, a record of 1.6 million food supplies were distributed to people in crisis while the number of UK food banks has also increased since 2010.

The Trust estimated that 14 million people have been living in poverty, including 4.5 million children.

Categories of homeless

While I agree with the basic premise of the Housing First approach that we will examine later, I do believe that you have the best chance of achieving success if you can house homeless people who are more likely to find the home appropriate for their onward progression.

One of the common complaints among HYP is that they find themselves among people with whom they have no commonality. A vulnerable young person who does not have any drug issues does not want to be with hardened addicts or people with a history of violence. Young people have a better chance of progressing with others of a similar age, rather than being in a hostel with people who have been out of mainstream society for decades.

It is also normally easier to concentrate support with people who have similar needs. Substance abuse schemes may be run on an individual and group basis. HYP who have a criminal record are likely to face similar problems in dealing with their past and how best to approach getting into work.

International comparisons

So how does the UK fare when compared to other nations? Habitat for Humanity estimated that, in 2015, 1.6 billion people around the world lived in 'inadequate shelter'.

The problem is that data is only available from certain countries and the information is based upon the estimates in Wikipedia and, again, may not include the hidden homeless, whom are a large proportion of the homeless population.

You have to seriously question some of the numbers when, as you may expect, North Korea reported not a single homeless person. Also, some of the world's trouble spots such as Syria and certain African countries (such as Somalia, Sudan and Ethiopia) or Myanmar were not on the list. Even if the true homeless numbers are likely to be higher, it provides some broad information to consider.

The UK recorded 307,000 homeless in 2016 at 0.46% of the total population. This percentage reflected one homeless person for every 200 in the country, excluding the hidden homeless. The UK recorded ratio was similar to Australia, but a number of European countries reported a lower homeless ratio, while the level of homelessness in some countries was staggering – Russia: five million (3.4%) in 2014 and Nigeria: 24.4 million (16.6%).[18]

The migrant crisis

Another area where I see no joined-up approach is the migrant crisis. The western world appeared to have been caught short by the huge migration of people fleeing war zones, as well as those looking for a better life, away from their country of birth.

The wars in Iraq, Syria, Libya and various countries in the African continent have resulted in millions of people being displaced. The response has been unstructured and inconsistent. The European policy of migrants seeking asylum in the nearest European country has put a huge strain on some of their members, while others have generally denied access and some countries, with an ageing population and a need for cheap labour, accepted larger numbers.

The issue was addressed by Alexander Betts and Paul Collier in their book 'Refuge: Transforming a Broken Refugee System'. They produced a number of well-constructed proposals that included housing refugees near to their home in economic centres that would enable them to return when the climate had improved, and so be part of the solution in rebuilding their country. Like many of the problems in the world today, we need a forward-looking plan that is most likely to provide a long-term solution, rather than a knee-jerk reaction that often creates as many problems as it solves.

Achieving success often requires the coming together of a number of different parties, from governments to companies that need encouragement to operate in areas that would not normally be

---

[18] Wikipedia

considered. Incentives need funding and can only go so far, and there has to be a will to be part of the process.

The youth homeless population

Having examined the total homeless population, how does that link with youth homelessness? It is the state's responsibility to house children who are homeless up to the age of 18 and so, for the purpose of this book, we are considering those in the 18-24 age group.

While those leaving the care system may initially get a helping hand, this will not last forever. In other cases, young people may become homeless after their 18th birthday. Councils across England, Scotland and Wales have released statistics that show that tens of thousands of young people have come forward to say they are either homeless or at risk of becoming homeless over the past year.

Figures from 234 councils obtained through a freedom of information request have lifted the lid on a hidden epidemic, with almost 45,000 18-24-year-olds approaching their local authority over the past year. However, with more than 100 local authorities not providing information, the real statistic could well be above 70,000.

Centrepoint estimated that 103,000 young people (aged 16-24) in the UK presented to their council in 2017/18 as they were homeless or at risk.[19] These young people were in crisis and often had nowhere to turn to beyond their local authority. However, again, this did not take into account HYP who did not present themselves to a local authority and were part of the hidden homeless population.

---

[19] Report 'Making homeless young people count: The scale of youth homelessness in the UK', Centrepoint.

Sage Foundation 2017 projected a much larger youth homeless population. It also mentioned that national figures only include statutory homelessness, and by excluding non-statutory and hidden homelessness, they fail to expose the full extent of the problem. Meanwhile, reductions in services for young homeless people have made tracking even more difficult. The report stated the following;

- 16-24-year-olds who are accepted as statutorily homeless made up just 12% (16,000) of the total number of young people that approach their local authority for support;
- Nearly double that number, 22% (30,000), will be turned away;
- These figures fail to account for the 'hidden homeless' – those who are living on the streets or just getting by on couch surfing with no guarantees of where they will sleep each night;
- On any one night, up to 255,000 young people are estimated to experience hidden homelessness – they are all at risk and need help.

The report further analysed the young homeless population as compared to the national population of young people:

- 46% of homeless young people are female;
- 24% identify as LGBT, compared with 3 to 4% nationally;
- 17% are children leaving care, compared with only 0.6% nationally;
- 56% are aged between 18 and 21.[20]

If we can better identify the youth homeless population and then keep track of those within this group, we have a better chance of permanently reducing this population. By way of comparison, a

---

[20] Report 'A place to call home – understanding youth homelessness' for Sage Foundation, Iesha Small, Ellie Mulcahy, Kate Bowen and Lolo Menzies, Sage Foundation, Fitzpatrick et al., 2017.

Canadian report (source: 'Supporting healthy and successful transitions to adulthood: a plan to prevent and reduce youth homelessness') reported that, in October 2014, a simultaneous point-in-time count was conducted in the seven largest cities in Alberta, Canada, and statistics were produced on the homeless and overall population.

The Canadian Government placed the number of homeless individuals in Canada at around 150,000 (inclusive of 65,000 homeless youth). This is a conservative number and some agencies estimate the homeless population to be between 200,000 and 300,000.

The current population of Canada is 36.7 million; just over half the UK population. If the Canadian experience is similar to the UK, it would infer that the Sage Foundation estimates may be nearer the mark.

Taking account of all the above research, I feel that a reasonable starting point is to assume a youth homeless population of 200,000 in the UK. While the total number is likely to be nearer 300,000, a proportion are likely to be less serious cases who may be able to struggle through to complete their education, find a job and move to an independent life.

On the basis that you have to start with a number of people whom you are confident are at risk and urgently need support, 200,000 would appear to be reasonable, based upon all that we currently know. So, later in this book, when we look at the resources needed to permanently reduce youth homelessness, I have based my calculations on a HYP population of 200,000.

As more HYP are identified and helped, the position should become clearer. Also, if measures are put in place to better identify the true levels of both core and wider homelessness among the youth, any strategic plan can be updated, and the actions required reconsidered.

The wider issues

Establishing the number of young people in crisis is one thing; having the resources to make significant inroads into permanently reducing youth homeless numbers is quite another. The lack of a central portal where HYP can go means that the system relies upon them making contact with organisations that they believe can, and will, help. Too often, HYP do not see the point of making contact in the first place. The government cuts have reduced the number of drop-in centres and outreach teams in the UK. These need to be built up again and financed at a sustainable level.

You then need enough well-trained support workers employed by the homeless charities who can handle their caseload in a way that enables them to provide a personalised service to each HYP on their books. The worker also needs access to specialist services covering the various support needs that we will examine in the next chapter. There is currently an insufficient supply of housing in the UK and, in particular, not enough homes for young people in crisis, and many of those that are available are temporary in nature and unsuitable.

There is also a critical shortfall of affordably priced move-on accommodation for those who are ready to live independently. There is an urgent need to help HYP catch up on any shortfall in their education, and then there is the issue of training for and achieving meaningful employment at a sustainable level.

The various problems faced by young people in crisis are not insurmountable and can be overcome in time, so long as a serious plan is created, with targets that are achievable and with the resources to achieve the goals set. The Brexit experience has made me sceptical about bland statements, wish lists and unachievable targets. I hope to show that a structured approach that brings together all aspects of society can make a real difference.

We will now examine the various support services that are needed, then look at the current state of play and the various parties that can bring a plan to fruition. This will show a role that we can all play in the process.

We will look at the matters to be considered when creating a home, with a view to transitioning young people from homelessness to an independent life, as well as the progress made by the residents. We will then examine the big picture in terms of funding and resourcing, and possible ways to achieving the ultimate aim of permanently reducing youth homelessness.

4

SUPPORT NEEDS

Overview

The various support needs for young homeless people often differ from those of the older homeless population. Every case is different, so it is important that systems are in place to cover the wide range of problems. The top 10 needs of young people accessing services are described in this chapter.[21]

The social fabric in the UK

There is clearly the need for a more intensive examination into the social fabric of this country, as the deep-seated problems that make life more difficult for many contribute to issues that ultimately give rise to homelessness.

An unexpected redundancy can push a parent into unemployment, creating financial hardship for the entire family, and ultimately, the loss of a home. Even those in work may be struggling to make ends meet, if wages have not kept pace with inflation. The knowledge that some nurses are having to go to food banks cannot be right.

A lack of future prospects, the drug trade in the UK and the rise in knife crime have driven young people into gangs, leading to

---

[21] Report 'Young & Homeless 2018', Homeless Link.

criminality. The cutback in benefits, reduction in money for social services and closures of drop-in centres and youth clubs all have an impact.

While prevention is better than cure, some of these issues are so complex and wide-ranging that they should be a priority for whatever government is in power, once politicians can concentrate on matters beyond Brexit. Even so, there is always likely to be a certain level of youth homelessness, as family relationships do break down, with adverse consequences for those involved, and problems related to mental health and substance abuse are on the rise.

Shelter reported that the highest concerns from overcrowded housing were the lack of privacy, the creation of stress, anxiety and depression in the home and not enough room for children to play, leading to arguments, fights, sleep disturbance and an inability to have friends in the home. Studying can become very difficult, leading to a poor education and subsequent employment prospects. In many cases, the situation becomes so bad that either the parent encourages an older child to leave or the child cannot take the living conditions and moves out.[22]

The economics help website www.economicshelp.com classified absolute poverty (where income is below the level necessary for basic living conditions) and relative poverty (where household income is 60% below median wages). The main causes of poverty are inequality in wages (low-skilled workers stuck in low-paid jobs), unemployment and long-term economic inactivity (no wage income, reliant on benefits), high renting costs, debt and debt repayments.

Unemployment has been the biggest cause of poverty in the UK. While there has been a relatively high employment rate in the UK, as compared to many other European countries, the rise in zero hours contracts creates a lack of security. A short number of hours

---

[22] Report 'Full house? How overcrowding affects families', Shelter fact sheet, 2007.

in a month can lead to individuals falling behind with rent and debt repayments; compounding their problems. This stressful situation can lead to mental health problems.

For a young person, starting out can be very difficult. Unless you are in a well-paid job from the outset, the income can be relatively low until you have established yourself. Expenses can be very high in proportion to your income. For those who cannot call upon the bank of mum and dad to help with a deposit for a home, renting is the only option, but in 2017, rent covered 27% of the salary in the UK, while in London, rent was as much as 49% of income.[23] Food costs have risen sharply, as have travel and other costs.

Young people need to earn enough to cover these expenses and, too often, the work can be sporadic, resulting in weeks when the income is not covering total costs. It is important that any homeless young person can move to a position whereby there is confidence that the income will cover all regular costs.

Budgeting knowledge and having the requisite life skills are important. A young person needs to have a financial margin of safety to offset any emergency outgoings. This is why sustainable employment is an important part of ensuring that a vulnerable young person does not fall back into homelessness at a later time.

Parents or caregivers no longer willing or able to provide accommodation

For the general homeless population, as for the young homeless, the problems associated with parents, relatives or friends no longer willing or able to provide accommodation is the most common theme, although for the youth, it reached 49% of cases, whereas for the general homeless population, it was 28%.

---

[23] Report 'How much of your salary is spent on rent?', Kevin Peachey and Daniele Palumbo, BBC News, 1st December 2017.

This can arise due to general poverty that has led to a parent not being able to support a youngster. Domestic violence could also result in a young person fleeing the family home. Criminality, substance abuse and mental health problems with the parent or child could have had an effect. Therefore one issue often links to another, so you could choose one of the other main reasons for young people accessing services that may relate to this heading.

Other significant causes of general homelessness include loss of rented or tied accommodation due to termination of assured shorthold tenancy (25%) and breakdown (both violent and non-violent) of relationship involving a partner. However, with youth homelessness, the other major causes were drug or alcohol problems (31%), mental or physical health problems (26%), leaving care (17%) and anti-social behaviour (17%).[24]

Therefore, if we are to help these young people, we need to ensure that the solution takes full account of these issues. Indeed, the severity of these problems can vary significantly from one person to the next.

Family mediation

The best form of prevention involves identification of problems at an early stage, such as in schools, where the signs can be identified. However, the pressure on schoolteachers and lack of training in matters of this kind are likely to result in early stage intervention being overlooked.

It may be possible to engage in counselling with all members of the family, to establish whether help can be provided to enable the abuser to change their behaviour sufficiently, so that the child can return to the family home. In some cases, it may be that the reaction of the child to the current environment has led to

---

[24] Report 'Young & Homeless 2018', Homeless Link.

anti-social behaviour that has had an adverse impact upon the other family members. Appropriate help could result in an eventual recovery of the family unit.

Various mediation models are used to support young people experiencing or at risk of homelessness. However, overall, the proportion of local authorities offering mediation declined from 92% in 2014 to 77% in 2015.[25]

Undertaken in the right way, mediation can be a useful tool to assist communication, thus resolve issues or disputes. Confidentiality is essential if mediation is to establish the cause of a dispute and provide a safe environment in which grievances can be aired. It may be necessary to use mediation alongside other services that may be required and not as a solution on its own.

In many cases, it may take an experienced and skilful mediator several sessions to help the parties identify the reasons for the family breakdown and find ways in which they feel confident to reunite. However research evidence highlights concerns that mediation is sometimes undertaken by housing officers who are not qualified family mediators, nor impartial, and may use it to drive a premature return to the home, as this can be recorded in prevention and relief data.[26]

A whole-family approach is important, as the breakdown often stems from complex issues affecting multiple people within the family unit. This requires a comprehensive service response, which often involves multiple agencies drawing on a number of funding streams. It enables the family to gain support as a unit, while recognising the importance of working with parents and children on a one-to-one basis.[27]

---

[25] Report 'Preventing youth homelessness: What works?', Centrepoint, 2015.
[26] As above.
[27] As above.

I have seen how one overseas charity has created accommodation units so that parents can visit the property that houses the child who has fled the family home. The counsellors work with all the relevant parties and have a high success rate in providing a better understanding of the issues that drove them apart and bringing them together, so that the child can safely return to the family home.

Domestic abuse

There were over two million cases of domestic abuse among 16-59-year-olds in England and Wales in the year to March 2018. Domestic abuse is not limited to physical violence. It can include repeated patterns of abusive behaviour to maintain power and control in a relationship.

The current definition of domestic violence and abuse recognises this and defines domestic abuse as: *'Any incident or pattern of incidents of controlling, coercive, threatening behaviour, violence or abuse between those aged 16 or over who are, or have been, intimate partners or family members regardless of gender or sexuality. It can encompass, but is not limited to psychological, physical, sexual, financial and emotional abuse.'*[28]

With the exception of coercive and controlling behaviour, which was introduced as a criminal offence on 29th December 2015, other acts of domestic abuse fall under generic offence categories in police recorded crime and criminal justice data, such as assault with injury.

As you can imagine, there are numerous situations that can lead to a young person fleeing the family home. On some occasions, it is through no fault of their own, while on others, they may have contributed, to a lesser or greater degree, to the impasse. Family mediation may be an important first step in the young person's

---

[28] The Office for National Statistics, Metropolitan Police.

rehabilitation, if there is a possibility of a return to the family home.

Mental health

Academics found that social and family context matters, as almost a quarter of 5 to 19-year-olds who had a mental health disorder were in a family that had been struggling to function well.

Professor Tamsin Ford, one of the research co-authors and a child psychiatrist at the University of Exeter, found that a variety of family adversities (such as parental separation or a financial crisis) or a child who has been socially isolated (with low levels of social support or not taking part in out of school activities) was also part of the explanation.

Those young people aged between 11 and 16 with a disorder were much more likely than their mentally untroubled peers to have taken illicit drugs, drunk alcohol or tried a cigarette. Among these children, the use of social media, widely blamed for causing much of the epidemic of poor mental health in young people, was also an important explanation. They are more likely to compare themselves with 'likes, comments and shares' on social media, impacting their mood.[29]

The following 10 statistics illustrate the level of mental health problems in the UK and their effect on young people:

- 16 million people in the UK experience a mental health illness;
- Three in four mental health illnesses start in childhood;
- 10% of school children have a diagnosable mental health illness;

---

[29] Article 'Top 8 reasons why teens try alcohol and drugs', The Partnership, '11 real reasons why teenagers experiment with drugs', https://drugabuse.com, 'Why do young people take drugs?', drugwise.org.uk, 13th February 2017.

- 75% of young people with a mental health illness are not receiving treatment;
- The average wait for effective treatment is 10 years after showing the first symptoms;
- Suicide is the biggest killer of young people in the UK;
- More than half of young people link mental illness with alienation and isolation;
- More than half of young people feel embarrassed about mental illness;
- Just 6% of UK health research goes on mental health;
- Less than 30% of mental health research is focused on young people.[30]

More recently, mental health issues have been covered by the media and it is hoped that this problem will be tackled more extensively, but we will have to wait to see what progress is made.

Charrissa's story was recorded on the St Mungo's website. It explained how the charity helped her to recover and shows how a normal life can quickly turn into a mental health problem caused by sudden homelessness.

"I became homeless after trying to rent a property that I found online. Everything seemed fine so I paid my deposit and first month's rent. A week after I moved in, the police knocked at my door. It turned out that the landlord was actually a squatter and was renting out the property illegally. The police didn't offer me any support, they just told me I had to leave, and I lost the deposit and the rent I had paid.

After I lost my flat I sofa surfed for a while, and then ended up sleeping under a stairwell in a friend's building for four months. I was worried about other people in the building complaining to the council and getting my friend evicted, so sometimes I stayed

---

[30] Post '12 statistics to get you thinking about mental health in young people', *The Guardian*, paid for by MQ: Transforming Mental Health.

outside. That scared me a lot. I remember spending a night on a park bench once, but it felt so dangerous I couldn't sleep.

I had to quit my part-time job because of travel costs, the stress of my situation and my depression – I just couldn't keep it up. I was homeless for about eight months in all. I kept going to the council for help but they just told me I didn't qualify as a priority.

It got to the point where I was really depressed, suicidal even. I kept thinking 'I've got a degree, how did I get here?' It was hard not having my family around".

As Neil of Oxford said,

"People with mental health problems are also portrayed as something you have to be afraid of because they're different, like homeless people are, but they are some of the most vulnerable and empathetic people you'll ever find..."[31]

Teenagers often experience emotional turmoil as their minds and bodies develop. An important part of growing up is working out and accepting your individual personality. Some young people find it hard to make this transition to adulthood and may experiment with alcohol, drug or other substances that can affect mental health.

Some of the more common mental health problems that can affect young people include:

- Depression;
- Self-harm;
- General anxiety disorder;
- Post-traumatic stress disorder – for example, following some form of abuse;
- Hyperactivity;
- Eating disorders.

---

[31] Report, 'Everybody in: How to end homelessness in Great Britain', Crisis, 2018.

The effect on the young person can vary greatly, depending upon the circumstances involved. For example, a care leaver may be well adjusted, if life in care had been well structured, providing sound life skills for adulthood. However, some care leavers may have had a varied and troubled childhood and may still suffer the mental scars from this experience.[32]

Particularly shocking was the report that 40% of homeless young people surveyed had experienced violence or abuse at home.[33] Given that 12% became homeless as a direct result of fleeing abuse from a family member, it is clear that some young victims of abuse were not receiving the right help and instead going on to experience homelessness.

Domestic violence is also a common experience for young homeless people. Overall, one in five of those surveyed had experienced violence from a partner. For young homeless women, though, the figure is much higher – 57% had been abused by their partner and in-depth interviews carried out by the researchers found that many had stayed in women's refuges at various times during their housing career.

Family abandonment is likely to have resulted in some form of mental health issue, ranging from low self-esteem to anger management and difficulty relating to people in authority, or peers. These problems may have led to other problems such as anti-social behaviour, crime or substance abuse.

For many young people, while a roof over their head is seen as vital, it is not always their first priority. Getting to grips with their personal circumstances and seeing a way forward can be a more pressing need.

---

[32] The Mental Health Foundation website, 2nd January 2019.
[33] Research briefing 'Young, hidden and homeless', Crisis, April 2012.

Trust is a key issue, especially if they have been let down by those who should have provided the support needed at this critical time in their lives. Often there has been no one constant person to whom they can turn. There may be no parent available, and if they have moved around, there may have been no one care worker to make a difference in their life. Even if they have remained in one area, the care team may have changed, so consistent support may have been missing.

What is needed at this time is a key support worker they respect. The winning of trust can take time, especially in cases where they have little experience of anyone who cares enough about their plight to have taken the time and effort to get to know them. Even when they are willing to trust enough to open up about their fears and concerns, they need a support network in place that has the skill sets to help. If there is one person who is the constant source of help, that is a very good start, but that key worker is likely to need to call upon experts in the different aspects of mental health.

Some issues may be deep-seated, while others may be easier to tackle. The feelings of shame and poor self-worth experienced by victims of physical or sexual abuse can be difficult to identify. It is only when a person feels close enough to someone that this subject is likely to be broached. The key worker will need to be empathetic and experienced in how to respond.

Those who have led a transient life due to abandonment or lack of a stable home, or have fled a war zone, may be finding it difficult to settle. Helping to overcome these feelings will need skill and patience.

Depression can take many forms and some behaviours may be hard to identify, whereas symptoms of attention deficit hyperactivity disorder (ADHD) tend to be noticed at an early age and may become more apparent when a child's circumstances change. The symptoms of ADHD usually improve with age, but many adults who were diagnosed with the condition at a young age may continue to experience problems later in life; possibly making it difficult when living with a new group of people.

Over the years, there has been a greater awareness of autism. Some extreme forms require a specialised unit, while individuals with mild forms of autism can live alongside non-autistic people, as long as their needs can be met.

Young homeless people with some form of mental health issue are likely to find that their condition worsens if they are not in an environment where the problems are identified at an early stage and treated appropriately. In too many cases, the emphasis has been in getting the young person off the streets, without dealing with the underlying cause of homelessness and the knock-on effects of the background experience.

Single homeless people are much more likely to have mental health problems than the general population. In 2015, 32% of single homeless people reported a mental health problem, and depression rates, for example, were over 10 times higher in the homeless population. Unfortunately, other psychological issues such as complex trauma, substance misuse and social exclusion were also common.[34]

Targeted prevention focused on this particular group of people is crucial. The homeless population struggle to access healthcare and tend to rely on A&E at crisis point, which was costing £85 million a year. In the words of Rick Henderson, chief executive of Homeless Link, we need more "multi-disciplinary NHS and housing teams who target housing, health and substance misuse in unison." They also reported that staff who work with homeless individuals in shelters, hostels or health services must be aware of their emotional and psychological needs and wellbeing, and put their safety first.

---

[34] Report 'Homelessness and mental health', The Mental Health Foundation, 10th December 2015.

Homelessness increases the risk of poor mental health, severe ill health and disability, lower educational attainment, long-term unemployment and poverty. There is no simple measure to resolve all of these problems, but the prevention of poor mental health is the key place to start. People cannot, and should not, be expected to make the journey out of homelessness without the right treatment and support.

The Big Issue report mentioned that mental ill-health was costing Britain £99 billion a year. It highlighted stark failings in provision for homeless people suffering from mental ill-health.[35] Research by homeless charity St. Mungo's found that four in 10 people who sleep rough in the south east need mental health support, with the figure rising to 50% across the UK as a whole. Studies also found that rough sleepers with psychiatric issues spend longer on the streets, with little or no effective targeted provision from mental health services, and that 40% of those surveyed had attempted suicide.

In the report, Isabel McCue (who established Theatre Nemo) said that studies have shown that a lot of addictions and poor mental health can be related to things that happened when they were children.

Over the past few years, there has been a greater awareness of mental health problems. Princes William and Harry have helped to publicise problems faced when they were younger and the media has certainly covered mental health more extensively. Mental health was often a taboo subject among some groups but is now more widely discussed. The use of therapists is also on the rise as people struggle to make sense of the problems they face and how best to cope. However, even where there is a will to help, there is often an incomplete structure to deal with the problems in

---

[35] Article 'Mental ill-health costs Britain £99 billion a year', Adam Forrest, *The Big Issue*, 26th October 2017.

a way that will result in a long-term improvement for young homeless people.

Substance abuse

Some of the reasons why young people take drugs include:

- Expectation – seeing parents or friends, taking drugs;
- Peer pressure – a bonding experience, especially among shy teenagers;
- Popular media – music, movies, TV making it 'seem cool';
- Escape and self-medication – from unhappiness, low self-esteem or depression;
- Boredom and curiosity – being alone and unoccupied;
- Rebellion – often against parents or circumstances;
- Instant gratification – seen as a short-term shortcut to happiness;
- Lack of confidence – to create a feeling of overcoming shyness etc.;
- Environment – drug supply in poor communities thrives;
- Weight loss – especially among female teenagers as a quick fix;[36]

Problems also arise with misinformation, from friends not providing the true facts about substance abuse. While drug use in poor communities has become big business and a way of life, it is also prevalent in our private schools and rural areas.

Research found that becoming homeless can lead to an escalation of drug use, in some cases. About 20% of young people reported that they began to use drugs after they became homeless; predominantly because it was the first time they had been exposed to them. Some young people who had previously used drugs

---

[36] Article 'Top 8 reasons why teens try alcohol and drugs', The Partnership, '11 real reasons why teenagers experiment with drugs', https://drugabuse.com, 'Why do young people take drugs?', drugwise.org.uk, 13th February 2017.

reported that they had used a greater variety since becoming homeless.

Substance misuse linked with homelessness can lead to begging and offending. Research also found that 95% of young people have committed an offence at some point in their lives. Of those, a quarter linked offences with alcohol use and half with drug use, and one third related offences to homelessness.[37]

Problems with drugs or alcohol can be part of a person's spiral into homelessness. Of course, not everyone who has problems with alcohol or drugs becomes homeless and not every homeless person has problems with drug or alcohol abuse. However, levels of drug and alcohol abuse are relatively high among the homeless population. In many cases, substance abuse is a result of homelessness rather than a cause. If dealt with at an early stage, the abuse can be overcome and not lead to addiction. Without a social support network, recovering from a substance addiction is very difficult. Often, people with untreated mental illnesses use street drugs as an inappropriate form of self-medication.[38]

While there was a general awareness of the danger of drug dependency leading to the use of substances such as heroin, the emergence of spice and other such substances is a worrying trend.

Research into factors associated with substance use among homeless young adults was carried out in the US in 2010.[39] A sample of homeless young adults aged 18-23 was recruited from a community drop-in centre and interviewed utilising self-report

---

[37] Fact sheet 'Young people and homelessness', Wincup E et al, Shelter, 2005. 'Youth Homelessness and substance abuse', report to the drugs and alcohol research unit, Home Office, London, 2003.

[38] Report, Crisis, 22nd March 2017.

[39] Research into factors associated with substance use among homeless young adults, Rebecca Gomez, L.C.S.W., Sanna J Thompson Ph. D. and Amanda N Barczyk M.S.W. of the University of Texas at Austin, School of Social Work, Austin, Texas, US, 31st January 2010.

instruments. Findings suggested that social networks, economic factors and future expectancies are significant predictors of the levels of substance use among homeless young adults. Being able to identify the areas that place homeless young adults at risk for substance abuse and dependence has implications for effective intervention.

Drug use among homeless young people was higher in comparison to their housed counterparts.[40] Substance abuse among this population has been reported as two to three times higher than found among non-homeless young adults. The stress resulting from sleeping outdoors and in public places may be alleviated or eased by using drugs and alcohol to keep warm and suppress hunger.[41] Some drugs were used to help these young people stay awake for extended periods; especially at night, when the chances of victimisation increased.[42] Drugs also provided a means of escape from the physical and emotional pain associated with surviving on the street.[43]

The research continued to report that although the stress of homelessness can increase the risk of substance abuse and dependence, some homeless young people overcome this vulnerability. Therefore, identifying factors that influence the severity of substance abuse among homeless young adults may assist service providers in tailoring treatment and services that maximise the strengths and resources of these young people.[44]

---

[40]   Article 'Rationale and Design of a Brief Substance Abuse Intervention for Homeless Adolescents', 'Addiction Research and Theory', Baer J S, Peterson P L, Wells E A, 2004,12 (4): 317-334.

[41]   Article 'Depression and Stress in Street Youth', Adolescence, Ayerst S L., 1999; 34 (134): 567-575, [PubMed] [Google Scholar].

[42]   As above and article 'Understanding street culture: A prevention perspective', Fest J., School Nurse News, 2003; 20(2): 16-18, [PubMed] [Google Scholar].

[43]   Article 'Disaffiliation, Substance Use and Exiting Homelessness', *Substance Use & Misuse*, 2003; Zlotnick C, Tam T, Robertson MJ 38(3-6): 577, [PubMed] [Google Scholar].

[44]   Article 'Correlates of Resilience in Homeless Adolescents', Rew L et al, Journal of Nursing Scholarship, 2001; 33(1): 33-40 [PubMed), [Google Scholar].

The research showed that the relationships between homeless young adults may provide a supportive function by protecting the individual, especially newly-homeless young adults, from the adversity of the street lifestyle. However, despite the benefits of homeless peer relationships, young adults often emulate the behaviour of their peer group, especially concerning substance misuse.[45]

In terms of a forward-looking approach, the research reported that evidence suggests that when adolescents perceive a high level of social support, their ability to understand that current actions have an impact on the future increases. This motivates them to engage in positive health practices.[46]

Results suggested that social networks, particularly peer networks, influence the level of alcohol use among homeless young adults. Those young people who had street friends who abstained from alcohol use also drank less frequently, whereas those whose peers abused or were dependent on drugs were also more likely to be substance dependent.[47]

In comparing homeless young adults who used, abused or were dependent on drugs, basic demographics are similar; however, peer influences appear to play a major role in youth's immersion in

---

[45] 'Capacity for Survival: Exploring Strengths of Homeless Street Youth', Bender K et al. Child Youth Care Forum. 2007; 36:25-42. [PubMed] [Google Scholar], Kipke MD, Unger JB. 'Street youth, their peer group affiliation and differences', Adolescence. 1997; 32(127):655 [PubMed] [Google Scholar], Dinges MM, Oetting ER. 'Similarity in drug use patterns between adolescents and their peers', Adolescence. 1993; 28(110); 253-266. [PubMed] [Google Scholar], Ennett ST, Bauman KE. 'Peer group structure and adolescent cigarette smoking: A social network analysis', Journal of Health and Social Behaviour. 1993; 34: 226-236. [PubMed] [Google Scholar].

[46] Article 'Alternate models of positive health practices in adolescents', Yarcheski A, Mahon NE, Yarcheski TJ, Nursing Research, 1997; 45(2):85, [PubMed] [Google Scholar].

[47] As above reference [45], Bender K et al.

the street environment, which is highly associated with use of illegal drugs.[48]

Criminality

A young person can be adversely affected by the geographical environment. For example, gang recruitment and petty crime can result in it being unsafe to stay at home, so lead to staying on acquaintances' sofas and rough sleeping. This can lead to anger management and other behavioural problems. What is needed is for someone to slowly help a young person to resolve these issues. A young person also needs to learn how to respect boundaries, set goals and deal with setbacks in a positive way; eventually getting to a stage where he or she is ready to move on and find a job.

The long-term danger for homeless young people is that minor anti-social behaviour can lead to criminality and a record that can significantly impact upon employment and general financial prospects later in life.

In Canada, young people were heavily at risk of becoming involved in criminal activities. Street youth, however, became involved in criminal activities to different degrees, ranging from not at all to high levels of participation. The types of offences they engaged in also varied, and included property crimes and distribution of drugs, as well as violent crimes such as robbery and physical altercations.

Research demonstrated that the road to the street often began with adversity in the home, including abuse, neglect, food insecurity and parental substance abuse, which leaves one at a

---

[48] Article 'Children in the streets of Brazil: Drug use, crime, violence, and HIV risks', 'Substance use & misuse', Inciardi JA, Surratt HL, 1998; 33(7): 1461-1480, [PubMed] [Google Scholar].

greater risk for criminal behaviour. This may be the result of weakened emotional attachments to guardians or from viewing the world as a coercive, hostile environment.

There was a strong link between some types of abuse and crime, such as physical abuse and violent offending. Those who experience particularly hostile abuse often see aggression as the way to solve problems and adopt values and attitudes that support the use of violence. Once leaving home, many youths also resort to crime as a means of survival, or to help cope with life on the streets.[49]

The Canadian research found that those who feel they do not have the capacity to cope with their homelessness by legal means are more likely to resort to crime and "situation adversity", or situations of desperate need (such as hunger) which can also have a direct impact on offending.

In the UK, Crisis explored the desperate measures that some homeless young people go to with a view to putting a roof over their head and not having to sleep rough.

It reported that 34% had committed a minor crime, such as shoplifting or anti-social behaviour, in the hope of being taken into custody for the night, and 17% had avoided bail or committed an imprisonable offence so that they would receive a custodial sentence, hence accommodation, while 18% attempted to admit themselves to A&E so as to be able to spend the night in hospital.

A high number of young people, particularly women, were forced into unwarranted sexual encounters – 11% had entered into a sexual partnership in order to get a bed for the night (for young

---

[49] Paper 'Why street youth become involved in crime', Stephen Baron, The Homeless Hub, Canada, included on page 356 of 'Youth Homelessness in Canada – Implications for Policy and Practice', 2013.

homeless women, this figure was slightly higher, at 14%). Shockingly, a quarter of young homeless women had engaged in sex work in order to fund accommodation or in the hope of getting a bed for the night.

The report highlighted one young boy, aged 14, who ran away from the family home and spent the next 10 years squatting, sleeping rough, and staying with friends on the odd night. He engaged in sex work on several occasions when he was 16, so that he could buy food and pay for a night in a B&B. It was only when he got in touch with a local housing association that he accessed the help and support he needed, after nearly 20 years of homelessness.[50]

The emergence of gangs in various districts around the UK has led many young people into a life of crime, especially when it becomes unsafe to stay at home.

In the US, surveys and experimental audits of employers have been conducted in recent years to understand how a criminal record affects future work. In the Milwaukee audit study, pairs of 'testers' were sent to apply for entry-level jobs – one applicant with a criminal record and one (otherwise identical) applicant without such a record.

For white testers, there was a large and significant effect of criminal record on employment: 34% of whites without records received call-backs, while 17% of testers with records received call-backs. For black testers, 14% without criminal records received call-backs, compared to 5% with a record. Thus, the effect of a criminal record was larger for blacks than whites.[51]

---

[50] Research briefing, 'Young, hidden and homeless, April 2012,' Crisis.
[51] Publication 'How work affects crime – and crime affects work – over the life course', Sarah Lageson and Christopher Uggen, Department of Sociology, University of Minnesota, 2013, Pager's (2003, 2007).

Unemployment among ex-criminals is not explicitly tracked by the US. Bureau of Labour Statistics but it was estimated at 27% in 2017 by the Prison Policy Initiative. However some researchers think it is even higher – informal estimates claim that as many as half of released convicts failed to find jobs or stayed out of the labour force.

Recently, more American companies such as McDonald's and Delta Air Lines have been hiring ex-convicts as part of their inclusion strategy. Executives said that 82% of their ex-offender hires had been at least successful as their average hire, according to a report by the Society of Human Resources Management. Only 14% of human resource managers would not consider hiring ex-offenders.[52]

In the UK, in 2011, the first detailed analysis of the criminal backgrounds of benefit claims showed that 33% of Britons claiming Jobseeker's Allowance had a criminal record. Three-quarters of people convicted in 2008 had made a claim for out-of-work benefits at some point over the previous two years, while almost half of those released from prison were still claiming unemployment benefits two years later. The total annual cost to the taxpayer was £8 billion.[53]

A UK report showed that in 2018, only 17% of offenders released from prison found work within a year. A new government strategy is incentivising businesses to help change that but prisons are worried that they will not have the capacity to carry it out properly.[54]

---

[52] Report 'Why companies are turning to ex-cons to fill slots in the US', Tim Mullaney, CNBC, September 2018.
[53] Article 'Third of unemployed are convicted criminals', Robert Winnett, political editor of *The Telegraph*, 28th December 2011.
[54] Report 'Why more ex-offenders may be about to be given a second chance', Colin Barras, BBC News, 27th August 2018.

Children leaving care

The state has an obligation to care for a child up to the age of 18 and after this age, personal adviser support is available to age 25. This is a critical transitional period in a young person's life. Despite the money spent every year on housing care leavers and homeless young people temporarily, too few young people are being supported with enough help to become independent. Funding is allocated to bed spaces and whoever fills them, so the support for young people does not go with them when it is time to leave.

One-third of care leavers experience homelessness in the first two years after leaving care. Housing providers and local authorities work hard to prepare young people to manage their future homes, but day to day, it tends to be easier and more time-efficient for key workers to take control. Subsequently, young people gain no experience of being independent before they have to do it for real, on their own. Sadly, as their main option for housing is now in the private rented sector, this inexperience often leads to eviction.

Education

When I started work, it was not unusual to find employment with one company until retirement. Now you cannot expect this form of security and the workplace continues to change in the UK. We have always been great engineers but our manufacturing base has shrunk over the years as the UK has built up its service industry in sectors such as finance and investment.

There has been a great change in the subjects that young people are studying. There continues to be a greater emphasis on the STEM subjects as the UK sees a greater market in the new world where science, technology, engineering and mathematics will be needed.

Certain sectors have recognised that they are under-resourced and steps are being taken to try to redress the balance. New schools are opening to offer young people from disadvantaged back-grounds the opportunity to study medicine as a reaction to the NHS personnel shortage.

The changes predicted for the future call for education to equip every young person with the appropriate set of skills. While academic skills such as mastery of reading, maths and science are important, there is an emerging need for young people to develop critical thinking and problem solving while empathising with others while working in a group. They need resilience and adaptability to continue to learn and master new problems.

An unfortunate by-product for many HYP who have suffered from family breakdown or other difficulties is the effect on their educational development. If you have fled home or been in severely overcrowded accommodation, the normal study pattern that most children enjoy may have not been available.

Young people can be very resilient, if given the opportunity. For example, in 2012, John Morris blogged about his experience.

"Since I was 16, after a brief spell with a mate's family, I've lived independently in supported housing. I'm 19 now, reading politics at Keele University. And so I've been wondering – am I some kind of exception?

A study by the Joseph Rowntree Foundation has shown a strong association between homelessness and withdrawal from education. But does this need to be the case? Can the young homeless not remain in education...?

Outside of accommodation, the most pressing issue for young people is their finances. I lived off benefits during sixth form; receiving £50 each week. This money had to pay for gas, electricity, rent, food, clothing, school equipment, travel and more. It was simply not enough. My education maintenance grant saved me, providing an extra £30. The EMA has now been cut. It needs reinstating, and the benefits system needs to be fairer to younger people. Under-25s do not get the full amount of income support, and under-21s get less money from part-time work. To help keep young people in education this ageist system needs an overhaul.

Universities need to offer more scholarships and bursaries for homeless students and realise the complexities of homelessness. These bursaries must be flexible, to stop students with unusual backgrounds falling between the cracks. Universities must also support homeless students during the holidays – they may be unable to find anywhere to stay. With the right support, there's no reason young homeless people cannot remain in education..."

Since that time, the Education Maintenance Allowance scheme has been closed in England. However, for those in care, a care leaver, a claimant of income support or employment and support allowance and either disability living allowance or personal independence payment, a bursary may be available from a school or college.

Further education or training is often an integral part of a young person's plan when they enter a home that is helping them move to independence. The challenge when working with HYP is to assess the best way for them to reach their potential, consider the most appropriate further education to suit their aims and abilities and support them as they get ready to complete their studies and join the jobs market. They need to believe that the education they need can be delivered and will bring about a positive change in their life.

The quality of the education received to date must be assessed at an early stage by someone who has the skills to identify any shortcomings that can prevent someone who is willing to do everything necessary to move on in life from maximising their potential.

Without wishing to curtail ambition, we need to be pragmatic about the future career for HYP as we support them to make the transition to independence. There seems to be a shift towards vocational training as the best way forward for many students and this may be the approach for many HYP to meet their aims and aspirations and the fastest route to the workplace.

Often, young people will be clear as to the path they want to tread whereas others may need more guidance as to the form of further education that will help them achieve the type of work that they will enjoy and take them to a place where they will succeed.

By discussing their strengths and aims, it is possible to develop an educational strategy that is likely to lead to a successful employment conclusion. It provides a better chance of success if the career chosen is in an area that is likely to be in demand for some years.

Employment

"Give a man a fish and you feed him for a day; teach a man to fish and you feed him for a lifetime" – (attributed to Maimonides).

Once a young person is ready to make the move to an independent life, employment (or self-employment) is one of the last pieces of the jigsaw.

A degree from a top university leading to a career as a solicitor in corporate restructuring is likely to result in a very high income and no lack of work. The biggest problem may be maintaining a reasonable lifestyle balance rather than earning enough money.

A job packing shelves in a supermarket or as a barista may be a start to get on the ladder but may result in joining the large number of those who are just managing to keep their heads above water and a change in market conditions, leading to job closures, could result in a return to homelessness.

Zero-hours contracts are trapping young people in homelessness, making it harder for 18-25-year-olds to escape homelessness and more likely for them to be saddled with rent arrears, leading to them being evicted. The result, said Jennifer Barnes, former head of policy and research at Centrepoint, was that young people trying to get back on their feet after having been homeless were effectively being penalised for 'doing the right thing' and getting a job.

"They have done what they are supposed to do, and it's not delivering for them," said Ms. Barnes. "We hear of people moving on from our services getting into trouble. They are desperate to get experience to improve their long-term prospects. They are being pushed by the Job Centre to take these zero-hours contracts. But if all they can access is a zero-hours contract, it will definitely be harder for them to escape homelessness in the long-term. These are young people who have already been through a lot. It's not the reward they deserve for doing the right thing."[55]

We live in a changing world where technology is seen as destroying jobs. However, this is far too negative a view, as you need to drill down to see what type of jobs it is automating and what type of work will be in demand. A 70-country study by the McKinsey Global Institute estimated that, by 2020, approximately 83 million high- and middle-skilled jobs will go unfilled because employers looking to hire in developed and developing countries will not find people with the necessary skills.

So while lower skilled jobs are being lost, technology is also creating more work – it is a case of looking at where the need is greatest. The dangers of the modern world are also opening up opportunities.

---

[55] Article on zero-hours contracts 'trapping young people in homelessness', Adam Lush, *The Independent*, 9th January 2017.

As we rely more heavily on internet trading, cybercrime prevention is becoming more important. It is leading many financial institutions to recruit bright young people who can help to build defence mechanisms. As we wake up to the dangers of climate change, there is a greater need to develop ways to live in a way that will protect the planet and find clean energy for business. The bleaching of coral reefs has led to creative thinking about how to regrow the reefs and encourage fish back to parts of the ocean that have become barren. As more rogue countries threaten terrorism, science and technology is being used to develop new methods to combat rocket attacks and track those who wish to carry out atrocities.

Looking further afield, we are trying to understand how artificial intelligence will change the workplace. An ageing population creates more problems to resolve. In Japan, the use of robots to help elderly people carry out basic functions is one approach but it cuts out the human contact that makes life worth living for some. Care workers are likely to be in demand for years to come and with the NHS under stress, opportunities arise in the nursing sector.

When planning a career, it is important to look ahead as to the likely source of demand. I have been in touch with a friend who is a good salesman and, as we know, in business, a company cannot make a profit if it cannot sell its products. However, the media advertising industry that he entered 20 years ago is very different today. It is often said that half of an advertising budget is useless; you just do not know which half. Companies are becoming more focused on how they drive business and what they spend to do so and he has found it much harder to earn a decent living in the advertising industry and is looking at other options.

The HYP that I have recently been working with have all identified areas where they should be able to find employment – care working, nursing and plumbing. These jobs are all valuable but generally not as well-paid as, for example, law or finance, and so they will need to be careful when budgeting their finances but at least they should be able to move on to an independent life once they complete their education. So, it is important that the young people can find their own way in life but also achieve sustainability.

There are many organisations that can help along the way. For example, homeless charities such as St Mungo's provide services such as:

- Accessing basic skills training to help with literacy and numeracy;
- Joining train and trade, offering courses on various trade skills, like bricklaying or decorating;
- Becoming employed by one of their partner organisations;
- Participating in a service with law firms to provide six months' paid work experience;
- Learning new skills in gardening and horticulture through the project funded by the Big Lottery Fund.

The Prince's Trust can help with developing skills and confidence as well as work experience. Three in four young people who complete their courses go into work, education or training. They also work with companies such as M&S, the NHS and Tesco. Help to develop CVs and interview techniques is also provided.

Many young people have ideas of their own for business and since 1983, The Prince's Trust has helped over 83,000 young people start their own business. They also help with their business plan and can tap into business experts for advice. Other charities have dedicated education and employment consultants who help on a one-to-one basis and also link with other organisations like The Prince's Trust or specialist employment training and advisory services companies.

There are a number of organisations that are helping homeless people in the UK at every step on the journey into employment:

- Change Please is empowering the homeless community by training them to be baristas – they also provide jobs paying

London Living Wage and support with housing, bank accounts and mental wellbeing;

- Beam is a crowdfunding campaign backed by various homeless charities to fund employment training for homeless people – users can sponsor homeless people and contribute towards training courses; they will then receive updates as they progress into employment;
- Timpson offers free dry cleaning for anyone who is unemployed and needs an outfit for an interview – all you need to do is go into the store and have a chat with one of their colleagues.

Benefits

There has been a great deal of media coverage over the cuts to benefits and the impact of benefit delays following the introduction of Universal Credit. Also, as with any state-run arrangement, bureaucracy can also create delays and hardship, which is why vulnerable young people need assistance on how best to take advantage of any finance that is available.

The benefit system can be complicated for the most knowledgeable adviser but a complete puzzle for HYP who may need assistance so as to obtain an understanding of the availability of financial support, what information and documents are needed to support a claim and help to follow through until the money is received. Many of the homeless charities can provide guidance as part of their support package.

The government's plan has been to bring the various state benefits together in the form of Universal Credit. While the idea was sensible, there was inadequate planning and resourcing, and this has led to confusion and delays in payment. The delays are worrying and can tip a person who is barely coping into home-lessness due to the absence of money to pay rent and other costs. The problems encountered have led the government to slow down the implementation of the Universal Credit roll-out programme.

Some of the main benefits that are relevant for HYP are the housing benefit, payments for supported accommodation, income support and Jobseeker's Allowance. In time, all of these payments are to be paid as Universal Credit. As part of the funding for a home, it is possible to arrange for the housing benefit to be paid to the landlord rather than the tenant, to cover the rent of a property. Any support income may be used to cover the costs of the various support services provided.

The potential for a supported accommodation payment will need to be discussed with the benefit department of the local authority but it can help with the funding of a scheme where a homeless charity is providing support services; possibly including live-in cover.

A young person needs to receive sufficient income each week to cover daily costs such as food and travel to college or work. Income support was set up to provide financial aid for those on low incomes who have not signed on as unemployed. A single HYP could receive £73.10 a week (£114.85 for a couple). The problem for many HYP is that it only applies if you are 25 or over. For a homeless young person, the level of income support or Jobseeker's Allowance has been in the £55-60 a week range.

The benefit system has understandably been set up to encourage a move into work and avoid benefit fraud but it can have unexpected consequences, so we have found that HYP need to have a good working knowledge of the benefit system before taking any action when embarking on their plans for the future.

I followed the plight of two HYP who were keen to take a part-time job to improve their English and job prospects while completing their basic education before studying for their chosen career. One part-time job paid £89.40 a week. The level of pay that applied before benefits were cut was £57.90 a week. As this was £31.50 over the limit, 65% of this figure i.e. £20.47 had to be put towards rent and could not be retained.

The HYP was unaware of the position until a couple of months later, when he received a letter informing him that the housing benefit paid to the landlord would be reduced by this £20.47 a week underpayment which, by then, had risen to £143; a large sum for someone who has little money and now faces eviction. Many HYP find the cost of accommodation extremely high before having any cut to benefits.

The position can get worse. If the part-time job ends or it is having an adverse effect upon studying, all benefits may be lost until proof can be provided that the right form of study, as prescribed for the HYP, is being followed.

It may be better to end the part-time job and concentrate on achieving the required further education. However, this requires confirmation from the local authority that the study being followed is within their guidelines. A new Universal Credit claim can be made if a HYP is in 'non-advanced education' (for example, studying for A levels or a BTEC National Diploma), is 21 or under and does not have parental support.

Moving into employment is obviously to be encouraged but, in some cases, it may be better to catch up on any basic education that may have been missed due to an unfortunate personal experience. The HYP may benefit by studying full-time for the necessary qualifications that will provide a better chance of securing a job that should produce a salary level to cover annual running costs and result in a move to independence.

I sympathise with staff working in the Benefits Department who have to calculate and pay money while protecting the taxpayer. When dealing with benefits due to HYP, I have found the system to be very complex and errors have arisen, as well as payment delays. This has all added to the financial problems faced by the homeless, as well as bureaucracy and time involvement for all concerned. I am aware of one case where there were nine separate letters from the Benefits Department over a 28-day period.

In the past, you would submit your tax return in paper form. Now, under self-assessment, you can go online and input the relevant information. The system then produces a tax computation that you can check, after which you can file your return. The system shows you how much tax is due and when it is payable, all without manual intervention from a tax inspector, while the same relevant information is available to you and the tax inspector. While the onus is on you to be truthful, HMRC can carry out a spot check at any time and demand all the documentary evidence for a tax year, with penalties for incorrect filing that produce under-declarations.

When it comes to the benefits system, I have found that there has been a great deal of unnecessary liaison with the Benefits Department to ensure that the correct money is received. Currently, you can establish how a Universal Credit benefit payment was made once it has been paid but not when submitting the information.

There is a balance to be struck between ensuring that there is no abuse of the system but that people in crisis can claim the benefits to which they are entitled in a timely manner and can plan their finances accordingly. When creating a home, keeping a cash buffer may be necessary; partly to overcome benefit delays. It seems that the benefits staff are suffering from a high volume of work and a system that needs further development.

Payments by card or bank transfer are becoming more common-place. Some sporting venues will only accept payments that can be made at the touch of a card, so as to avoid crowd delays. While we have not yet reached the time when cash is no longer used, it is likely to be the way forward. The move from cash payments should also reduce tax avoidance and increase revenue for the Exchequer. It could also open up the opportunity for more inte-grated systems if tax and benefit avoidance through cash pay-ments are of less concern to the government.

The further development of the benefit system that enables online data input and benefit calculation at the time of submission of information, similar to the self-assessment tax system, should enable a HYP to provide the relevant information to enable the benefits to be loaded online, computed online and paid, with a much reduced administrative burden. Spot checks can be carried out periodically and the benefit department can check the receipts as shown by the bank account. No doubt there will be various data protection, security and other issues to overcome before we have a system that is user-friendly for all concerned.

Life skills

As we have seen, there may have been a number of reasons why a young person is homeless; many of which may have resulted from a chaotic upbringing that has left gaps in their ability to survive in the wider world, as compared to those from a more conventional background.

They may now be in the right mental state to move on from homelessness but may not have the requisite life skills that many take for granted. These can be regarded in terms of broad categories, such as:

- Core skills – numeracy, literacy and information technology;
- Independent living skills – managing a household, budgeting, cooking, appointment keeping, contacting services, dealing with bills and correspondence;
- Social skills – interpersonal skills, dealing with neighbour disputes, effective communication, developing self-confidence and social networks;
- Employment skills – CV creation, interview techniques, time management, problem solving, goal setting, teamwork, organisation and conflict resolution.

Life skills training is different from support, help or assistance, in that the aim is to promote self-sufficiency. It is important that any training is tailored to the specific needs of the individual and takes account of the level of training required. It is also important to identify an individual's aspirations before planning a way to achieve them.

Literacy tutor for St Mungo's, Simon Phillips, said that one of the biggest challenges can be to reach people who have been failed by the education system in some way as they may have an instinctive resistance to anything that looks like traditional education. This can be overcome by showing the skills that are relevant to them and how they can be acquired. He believes that the impact of the work can be dramatic, especially when you are helping a small group, say no more than 10 people, over about six months. It is not just about getting people back into work, it is about giving people the capabilities to do what they value in life.

The DePaul website illustrated the case of Tanya who, at 17, was asked to leave the family home. She was argumentative and felt that no one believed in her, had no confidence, low self-esteem and suffered with anxiety and depression. At a hostel, she was not responsible, got into debt, did not keep appointments and was not motivated.

When Tanya moved into a shared house, she was not taking responsibility for cleaning or paying her bills. She turned her life around when she met a DePaul support worker and, for the first time, felt that someone was listening to her. They helped her with the skills she needed and she is now doing well, paying her rent, no longer in debt, motivated, happy, and will soon be moving into her own home.

I noticed one of the subtle ways in which life skills can be taught in a small group in the case of one home that housed several young people, whom had previously been homeless, with a full-time, live-in key worker. The residents generally got on well but when one had an issue, he would approach the key worker and ask that the problem be solved.

In this case, the key worker would gently explain that the resident needed to take up the matter himself and help by showing how this could be achieved. Once a young person had successfully overcome a problem of this kind, it provided the platform to appropriately deal with similar situations that may arise.

Even when a HYP has employment at a reasonable level, basic financial planning skills should be in place to avoid that person overspending and falling into a downward spiral of not being able to meet regular monthly costs; possibly leading to a loss of accommodation and a route back to homelessness. While circumstances such as unemployment and benefit cuts may be unavoidable, the HYP should move to independence with the necessary tools to avoid adding to problems by financial recklessness, as far as possible.

Renting accommodation

A homeless young person may be employed and ready to move into rented accommodation but is likely to have no experience of the process or know the potential pitfalls. The Shelter website provides some good tips for first-time renters, including:

- Don't pay letting agents to register;
- Be sure it's safe, including checking the gas safety certificate;
- Check that your deposit will be protected;
- Make sure the inventory is accurate;
- Know your own responsibilities;
- Check you understand any agreements (including joint tenancies);
- Check the procedures if your landlord wants to increase the rent;
- Check who is responsible when things go wrong e.g. the boiler breaks down;
- Check the procedures required when you are ready to leave;
- Make sure you can get your deposit back.

The Citizens Advice Bureau can also be helpful in providing advice on what needs to be paid up-front so that you do not get a shock and can assist with benefits-related issues.

Mentoring

We generally do not receive training in how to retire. Where once a person may have been an important cog in the corporate wheel, he or she now has more time available, but for what purpose? Some are happy to spend the day gardening, playing golf or engaging in another hobby. Others find that they have suddenly lost their purpose and can become lethargic. Often, these recent retirees have a great deal of expertise that is going to waste. However, HYP may be greatly in need of the type of help that can be provided.

If we look at the list of needs that HYP have, there are a number of ways in which mentoring can help while that person is in a homeless state, and afterwards, when that person has moved to independence.

Some of my friends have taken retirement as an opportunity to train for work that they always wanted to do, such as counselling and family mediation, or help with a HYP's mental health. Those who have suffered in the past from substance abuse and have been clean for years could be a source of inspiration and help to those still using drugs.

Retired teachers could be of great benefit to those who have lost out due to a chaotic upbringing. Retirees from a business or social services background could be of assistance, especially if they were in the sector being considered by the young person. While there are charities that help young people prepare for interviews, a mentor who can stay with the young person on a one-to-one basis can be a great support. Even when a person has found employment, the mentoring process does not necessarily stop.

There are numerous examples of a need for mentors to help HYP with life skills. Accountants can help them develop an understanding of finance and budgeting. A decent cook could help young people who have never had to make their own meal. IT skills are becoming more important at work, or in life generally. Retired consultants on time management and organisation have a role to play.

Problems at work can be discussed with a mentor to find the best approach to solve issues that may seem small to an experienced businessman but insurmountable to an inexperienced employee. There are many people who have a great deal of valuable experience and could become a huge help for a young person to turn to, with a view to taking early steps to avoid falling back into the homeless trap.

I recall the case of a young man in his 40s who was mentored by an older retired adviser. Even after a decade, he still calls to discuss how best to approach issues at work so as to ensure that he can maximise his potential, enjoy the salary that he needs and take action where appropriate if he is not getting the right reward for his efforts. The discussions have covered alternative job offers that were often not as attractive as they first seemed and the mentor has steered him in a positive way that maximises security for his family. It has been a successful relationship for both, who have benefited from working through the issues that have arisen.

Causal links

There are numerous links from one cause of homelessness to another. In many cases, the homeless person will have suffered from a number of issues that, at first glance, do not appear to be related. There can be family breakdown, poverty, depression, drug taking, mental health issues, knife crime and criminality.

In the few cases that have been covered, you can see how problems that started with a rogue landlord spiralled into depression, mental health issues and suicidal thoughts. The psychological torture of homelessness was described, as well as how easily it can lead to substance abuse. The difficulties of getting employment without an address or cleanliness were explained. We also saw how domestic abuse can lead to homelessness, with the dangers that can result, and how the geography of where you live can put you in peril with street gangs. It starts to illustrate the complexity of this subject and how merely putting a roof over a young person's head is not going to solve the problem.

PART II

TAKING STOCK

'If we carry on as we are, homelessness in Britain is expected to double in the next twenty-five years'.

Source: Crisis report 'Everybody in: How to end homelessness in Great Britain' (2018).

5

THE CURRENT POSITION

Background

Having provided some background to the current plight of homeless young people in the UK, we can now look at some of the deficiencies in the provision of support and then consider what can be done at a micro level, explore the roles that can be played by the government, homeless charities, the private sector and individuals and then examine what is needed to significantly reduce youth homelessness in the UK.

Perception and reality

The major newspapers covered this social problem, as did the BBC and radio stations such as LBC. However, as indicated at the start of this book, there is still a public perception of homelessness that is both factually incorrect and unhelpful. Much work is needed to illustrate the true position and that may mean various charities working with creative advisers and the media. It is hoped that this will lead to a greater understanding of the issues, a better engaged public and more support from potential funders from the private sector.

Scale of the problem

If we carry on as we are, homelessness in Britain is expected to almost double in the next 25 years.[56] With a homeless situation

---

[56] Report 'Everybody in: How to end youth homelessness in Great Britain', Crisis, 2018.

that is currently unacceptable, this should give rise to priority action, but there are so many other matters that are of concern (such as support for the NHS) that we need to be realistic about what can be achieved and take a new approach to make serious progress.

A starting point

Where does a HYP go to start the process of getting help? The starting point is often the local authority. However, the local authority would firstly want to establish whether the individual qualifies for help at this time and many may not fall within this category. Even if help is due, the quality of support may differ from region to region.

As we will consider later, too often, HYP are faced with an institutionalised approach that concentrates on the perceived problems rather than getting to the root of the matter. Sending someone for anger management control does not solve the problem of why anger is expressed if there is no understanding of the abuse at an earlier time.

My understanding is that staff often do not have the required skills to really understand the scope of the issues experienced by the HYP. This may only arise when an experienced counsellor establishes trust, and this takes time. Even if the local authority has got to the root of the problems, it is likely that the HYP will be passed on for help with accommodation to one party and support services to another or to multiple organisations.

As a community agency stakeholder in Edmonton, Canada, said, "Youth don't want to tell their story 15 times – they need one single point of entry into the system."

The London Youth Gateway is a partnership between New Horizon Youth Centre, Depaul: Alone in London, Depaul Nightstop, Shelter and LGBT Jigsaw; all established providers of services to homeless young people. Funded by London Councils, the partnership combines the resources of a day centre, specialist youth homelessness advice services, emergency and longer term accommodation, a telephone advice line and LGBT service providers. As such, it offers precisely the kind of youth-focused, holistic and tailored advice and support that young people need but often struggle to access – including the many who are 'non-priority homeless' but who urgently need help.

Because of the partnership approach, a young person can use different services across the London Youth Gateway depending on their specific needs and circumstances, no matter which one they access first.

The London Youth Gateway offers holistic support to young people in housing need, covering:

- Accommodation advice and support;
- Homelessness prevention;
- Education, training and employment;
- Emotional and physical wellbeing.

Once a HYP gets to a London Youth Gateway charity, I would expect them to get the best opportunity to progress, but how easy is it for someone who has just become homeless, for example, having fled the family home, to find the person or organisation that will be the best fit?

A 'single front door' approach is utilised by many local authorities as a gateway into services. This may be a physical hub building where agencies are co-located and facilitate access to other services within the pathway. Due to the chaotic nature in which this group of young people engage with services, often shifting between home and homelessness, the single front door streamlines and simplifies their engagement. Much like multi-agency working, it also enables practitioners to coordinate a holistic package across a range of services and reduces the risk of a young person falling between these provisions.[57]

I expected to find more drop-in centres for HYP as these can prove to be an important first step to gaining the help needed to move on from homelessness and start addressing the action needed to make progress towards independence. I have been told, on various occasions, that the government cuts and general lack of funding have resulted in drop-in centres being closed. These centres are an important part of the infrastructure needed and can work well with permanent housing for HYP.

Centrepoint operates a helpline (https://centrepoint.org.uk/helpline) and recommends that Central Government should sponsor a national, virtual portal giving all young people access to advice and information about homelessness. This portal should facilitate access to homelessness services in the young person's local area, in partnership with local authorities.

The Centrepoint recommendation should be adopted as part of a business plan to reduce youth homelessness but it is only a part of what is needed and, in particular, how the resources are to be put in place and how they will develop.

Data collection

When seeking information about the number of HYP in the UK, I found that many organisations sought to quantify the problem but were restricted by a lack of accurate information. As we have seen, if we are to make serious inroads into the youth homeless problem, we need more accurate information and a linkage between the various organisations that are contacted by HYP, such as local authorities and homeless charities.

---

[57] Report 'Preventing youth homelessness: What works?', Centrepoint, 2016.

A 2018 Canadian report stated that the development of a data collection system is important in collecting baseline data, determining the scope of the issue, providing information on evidence-based programming and identifying community need or gaps in support. Data collection on homeless youth will ensure that programmes and services are efficient in their operation and will help to measure outcomes. Its action plans included:

- Working with youth shelter providers to implement a Homeless Management Information System.
- Establishing information sharing arrangements with youth-serving organisations to facilitate the single point of entry system.[58]

In this advanced technological age, I would have thought that security measures could be put in place so that all organisations involved with HYP can log and share the necessary information.

An integrated approach

To provide a solution to a HYP, it is necessary to create a home rather than short-term accommodation and provide a range of services that are tailored to the individual's needs, including preparation for an independent life and move-on accommodation. Too often, the emphasis has been to get a person off the streets but the accommodation provided is not conducive to enable progress to be made, and the services are not provided in a manner that is likely to produce the best results and the fastest transition to independence.

Accommodation

The next section will look at the different types of accommodation currently used to house HYP; clearly the structure of many of these properties does not help in allowing HYP to progress. Later,

---

[58] Report 'Supporting healthy and successful transitions to adulthood: A plan to prevent and reduce youth homelessness', Alberta, Canada, 2018.

we will look at other options: what can be achieved to free up properties in the short-term, how a sufficient number of appropriate properties can be built over the longer term and meet the need for affordable move-on accommodation.

Support needs

The support needs have been covered earlier but often there has been an insufficient number of skilled consultants to provide what is required. The training for people coming into the homeless sector should be improved. Many people are experienced through practical work over time but did not have the requisite training from the outset. We need to start thinking long-term about how we recruit and train the next generation of support workers and the courses at college and university that can best provide the academic training prior to taking on a practical role in the homeless support sector.

When it comes to the support services, it is not only the quantity of support providers but also the quality of support needs and approach taken that can vary greatly. A somewhat institutionalised rather than personalised approach can lead to poor outcomes.

The problem, in my view, is that the quality of support is very mixed. There are many dedicated and talented staff working extremely hard in trying circumstances, as the demands upon them can be very high. In other cases, the constraints to which they work make it hard to provide the HYP with the personalised support that they need.

Resident mix

As a consultation participant in Leicester reported, "People with different needs all end up in the same place – offenders, drug and alcohol users and people who are not. It is unsafe, chaotic, people get robbed, bullied – especially if they are vulnerable with special needs, young, not streetwise."

The selection of residents in a home is very important as, ideally, you want to see both the individuals and the group prosper. You are likely to achieve greater success if you select the group while taking account of the severity of needs and personalities. A wrong mix can lead to chaos while a good mix can produce a self-help group, some of whom may stay in touch after they leave a home.

However, this is not to say that you need to categorise the residents too rigidly, as young offenders can live with others, if they buy into the rules of the house and there is confidence that they will not be a seriously disruptive or negative influence. Indeed, in some cases, it can be beneficial to include a HYP who has different needs and support.

The charity sector

There are a large number of charities competing for funding that may not always be conducive to a close working relationship. We need to examine how many HYP charities are able to take on the work and what steps may need to be put in place to cope.

The charities that are succeeding in providing the right level of help for HYP need greater funding so that they can expand their services. Many are concerned by the donations needed each year and do not have enough money coming in annually, so are constantly worried about whether they can sustain the current services at a time when the demand is rising.

The state

The Homeless Reduction Act 2017 provides a number of helpful measures but unless there is a coordinated approach involving the government and other parties, the aims of reducing youth homelessness are unlikely to be achieved.

With the competing funding requirements of the NHS, state pension and other state outgoings, we need to be realistic about what can be achieved; especially in view of the public debt and lack of focus in recent years. This will be explored further in more detail.

Different approaches

We can learn from people who have sought to tackle social issues when considering how other nations have found different ways to reduce youth homelessness.

Closer to home, Scotland has been successful in reducing knife crime and rough sleeping, although homelessness has, again, been on the rise, of late. The Scottish Centre for Conflict Resolution provided families with support and advice on how to solve problems. As family breakdown is a key reason for youth homelessness, this is a good approach in preventing a problem from expanding into the need for a cure.

In the UK, there are many charities seeking to tackle homelessness. Some provide accommodation but outsource the support services, some have in-house key workers while others have floating support, and some organisations seek to provide a comprehensive solution while others home in on certain aspects and outsource other services.

The local authority approaches differ from region to region in regards to their terms and the benefits that they can provide. Some local authorities have created partnerships with certain charities for young people from a particular background, such as care leavers, whereas others may be more willing to work with a broader range of charities.

In some ways, this localised approach can preclude certain initiatives from developing, while in other cases it provides an opportunity for a charity to widen its sphere of operations and lead the way.

A starting position

Clearly prevention is better than cure but even if we were working on a cure for a homeless person, it is best to ensure that the medicine will work and be effective.

Centrepoint has completed separate research ('Preventing youth homelessness: What works?') to explore the potential public savings that could be gained from preventing homelessness before young people reach such a crisis point. If prevention at an earlier stage could produce significant financial savings for local authorities and central government, then there is a clear incentive to increase the funding for early intervention programmes for young people at risk of homelessness.

The study estimated the net public cost of a young person experiencing homelessness by comparing the public costs of NEET (not in employment, education or training) young people to people who are both NEET and homeless. The cost of a NEET young person aged 18-24 was £7,200 while the cost of a NEET homeless young person in that age group was £19,400; thereby putting the added cost of homelessness at £12,200.

A fully structured business plan that will meet the cost of homeless reduction should be a starting point. It could include representatives from each group that should be involved in the process, setting out roles and targets for each. It can then measure the outcomes against the targets set.

There are likely to be different initiatives and entrepreneurial approaches if we are to be successful in achieving homeless reduction targets and maintaining a much lower level of homelessness in the UK. However, a national plan will need to take account of the current array of available providers of services and include all the various initiatives so that they can be monitored on an individual basis to see how successful they are, identify any problems and consider how they can be solved. This should also enable us to learn from new initiatives that are working well.

6

ACCOMMODATION

Homeless accommodation

Creating the right form of accommodation is essential in providing an appropriate environment for HYP to progress. Unfortunately, this is not the case for most young people, as we will see.

There are various forms of inappropriate accommodation used by HYP, and this will have to change. With a youth homeless population of 200,000, this will require a combination of converting existing housing and creating new homes of different structures and sizes.

Rough sleeping

The misery of sleeping rough was illustrated earlier, and clearly HYP urgently need to get off the streets and receive the support required to help them move to an independent life. While rough sleeping is a small part of the overall homeless population, it is the most visible and perhaps the most dangerous.

Sleeping in cars and buses

A YouTube video by Jody on 19th July 2017 illustrated her plight. She joined the military at 19 but due to mental and physical health issues arising from her service, she needed treatment that led to her leaving her job and then selling her house to make ends meet.

With nothing left, she felt that she had no choice but to sleep in a vehicle. She talked about the misery of waking up with no toilet, shower or hot food.

The BBC reported the growing plight of homeless people sleeping on buses as they felt safer than on the streets (29th October 2018). However, sleep is not easy, because at the end of the bus route, you are required to get off and have to wait until you can get back on again for the return journey. Transport for London has linked with Thames Reach in an attempt to help, but it shows the lengths that homeless people will turn to in an attempt to get off the streets.

Squatting

Squatting is defined as someone deliberately entering a property without permission and living there or intending to live there; sometimes known as 'adverse possession'. Squatting in residential buildings (like a house or flat) is illegal and can lead to six months in prison, a £5,000 fine or both. Squatting in a non-residential building is not, in itself, a crime, unlike refusing to leave on the orders of a Court.

Squats can be chaotic places but need not always be so. Declan Cashin, on 30th October 2018, for Housing Week and the BBC, interviewed Chris, an unemployed chef and a key figure in a large squat that housed 20 homeless people in Manchester. Chris explained, *"The youngest in the group is age 17, and the majority are in their 20s and 30s. There are three basic rules for everyone: no taking hard drugs, no constant drinking, no abuse in any form. You break any of those rules, you're out the door.*

A squat may not be a typical house-share but it works on the same basis. It's give and take all round among those of us in a squat. People share everything, not just the chores. We share everything from emotional support and advice to money and clothes – everything is about building that family, that support network rather than trying to outbid or outdo each other. The whole idea behind it is so they take pride in the building, pride in themselves, pride in the family unit.

Everyone in the squat is responsible for everything in the squat – collecting the rubbish, going skip-diving for food, and reaching out to other groups for supplies. We run the squat as a home, so the whole ethos I try to instil in people is – treat it like your home, respect the place like your home. We tend not to fall out over politics – the general view is: whoever you vote for, you're getting screwed.

We have had to ask people to leave the squat before but rather than just turfing someone out, we try to place them in other squats, places that have different rules and values. It doesn't work every time. Sometimes people don't want to change, and there's nothing you can do about that. You give people leeway, but if that person is causing unrest in the house, then that person needs to go.

I feel that people have undiagnosed PTSD from sleeping rough. It's very emotional. So when they come into a squat, and are given responsibility for themselves and others, some people can't deal with it. When they leave, we say to them – we're still here for you. We're still your family, still your friends."

It was subsequently reported that bailiffs and police, acting on a High Court order, removed Chris and the other squatters. Two days after the eviction, Chris said, *"Everyone evicted from the squat is still with me. We're all together in another squat. We now have twenty people bedding down in a room that's only fit for ten."*

Hostels

The hostel system is a very large response to homelessness. It focuses on single homeless people. At the time of writing, there are approximately 1,121 projects providing 34,947 bed-spaces of accommodation (a decrease of 3% since 2016). Just over half the projects (580) range between one and 19 beds in size. However, 541 accommodation services are 20 units or greater in size and 161 projects are over 50 beds in size. This level of communal sharing can be stressful and difficult to manage for people with mental health problems or other support needs.

When 108 people were interviewed, only two people stated that they wanted to live in a homeless hostel. In two separate focus groups, the consensus was that people would prefer to be in prison rather than in a hostel. Resistance to moving into hostels was consistent. They explained that the chaotic environment, poor quality accommodation and limited opportunities for moving on were key deterrents.

Over the past 10 years, hostels and supported housing units have been generally decreasing in size. More than half the projects in England have 20 bed spaces or fewer, providing a more personalised form of support.

Hostels and supported housing schemes are expensive, with average weekly rates of £171, £179 and £199 in England, Wales and Scotland respectively. A Great Britain average weekly rate was noted to be £175. This is considerably higher than the cost of mainstream housing. These costs are associated with higher maintenance, repairs and renewals, the provision of communal facilities and health and safety costs, higher housing management and the nature of capital funding arrangements. The larger services require 24-hour staffing to ensure that support for residents is provided, access arrangements so that residents can get in immediately and building security and maintenance.[59]

The Big Issue, 5th July 2016, carried the story of Jason Petch, who illustrated what life can be like in a hostel.

---

[59] Report 'Everybody in: How to end youth homelessness in Great Britain', Crisis, 2018.

After becoming homeless, Jason moved into a hostel but he says that the system is blighted by wasted money and wasted lives. He did not want to name the hostel for fear of receiving a 14-day notice, as his only other option was sleeping rough.

He challenged the rent of £991 a month, which he regarded as extortionate for services of hot water, shared bathrooms and toilets, electric, heating, and two meals a day (breakfast and an evening meal). There is a subsidised launderette where it costs £2 for a wash and dry, which he regarded as good value, and once a week, clean sheets are provided by the hostel.

Jason had access to a support worker who had approximately 40 pages to fill in for each new arrival and felt that proper counselling and rehabilitation could give these human beings a real shot to change their lives.

He said *"I had lived on benefits since losing my job. The local council paid £863.20 in housing benefit and the tenant was then responsible for the remaining balance out of their benefits. A one or two-bedroom flat in our city can be privately rented for around £350-£400 per month.*

There are many private landlords looking for tenants so why can't the local council and the charities concerned have their heads screwed on tight and begin to rent local private landlords' homes and help homeless customers with their deposit in real time? The council could then save itself £55,000 per month for all 117 residents. Proper counselling and rehabilitation could give these human beings a real shot to change their lives.

Homelessness is treated as nothing short of a disease. The individuals here in the hostel are classed as citizens that aren't worth the title human being. I am not saying that they do no good work but they do not give respect to the human beings living here.

I know that some homeless people are dealing with drug and alcohol abuse, prostitution and anything else that can be done to survive. The reason is: they have become a statistic. They have become immune to a life worth living and just inhabit a space of self-existence.

The worst aspect of the place is where our room is situated. There is a flat roof directly outside, littered with foil, hypodermic needles and other drugs paraphernalia. I have never been a drug user and I have never abused alcohol but I understand the difficulties involved and the complex choices behind addiction. What I have not seen here is a proper support system, a system where they really get the masses of support to enable a life free from addiction.

Again the reason is cost. The local newspaper published an article in September 2015, which stated that the city council spends £9.6m per year on their substance misuse programme, which treats 2,705 people, with 1,676 being given methadone and buprenorphine. So that works out as £3,548.98 each, on average. This times, say, 100 people out of 117 and you have a very hefty bill.

I hear the voices of approximately fifty per cent of these tortured souls asking for help, please help us. Do they mean it? Absolutely. This complaining, as the staff see it, falls on deaf ears. Why aren't we truly helping these individuals to return to a life worth living? Why are we constantly ignoring these issues?

What really breaks my heart is kids between the ages of 16 and 25. These youngsters should be living life to the absolute fullest. They need to know they are valued and not just a menace to society. I know they shouldn't steal and do the atrocious things they do to get money for their addiction. I am not condoning this behaviour in any way, shape or form. However, I can understand why they do. They aren't saints, they are real characters.

I truly enjoy so many of these incredible people's stories. I see the injustice and am right there living it alongside them. I hear you say that they can only be helped if they want to be helped. Well, maybe it's incredibly scary to stand up and say this isn't a life I want to live any more. I hear many people say it but they are passed over as being unable to accept help. It is time to break the class culture and to also give respect to those who struggle in life, rather than create a wall of ignorance around them."

In some areas of the country, there are beds available for the homeless but people with comparatively low needs do not want to be with people with high needs and, in particular, those with serious substance abuse or mental health problems. Some people are worried about being mugged in a hostel and would rather sleep rough.

Winter shelters

Homeless Link provides information on the range of winter shelters (or cold weather shelters) that operate in London each winter. Some open just for a week over Christmas, others are open for several months. They vary in size, from about 10-40 spaces, although Crisis at Christmas accommodates several hundred people.

A lot of the shelters listed are organised by local church or faith-based groups and operate in a different church hall or community space each night on a rota basis. Details of the venue for the night are given when someone is offered a place.

The shelters are usually staffed by volunteers, offer basic accommodation in communal sleeping areas and provide breakfast and an evening meal. There is not usually a charge for staying in the shelter.

Placement in a winter shelter is usually done on a referral basis and often coordinated by one local organisation. Although they may take referrals directly from homeless individuals or from any agency, there may be an expectation that a referring agency will be responsible for providing ongoing support to the person and helping with their onward move.

Domestic abuse survivors in refuges

While women and children are not the only survivors of abuse, they are the largest group in this category. Women's Aid reported that, in 2017, there were 229 providers providing 365 local domestic abuse services throughout England. Based on answers to the Women's Aid Annual Survey 2017, they estimated that they were 3,557 with 3,919 children and young people staying in refuge. Over the year 2016/7, refuge services supported a total of 13,414 women with 14,353 children and young people across all services in England (Women's Aid, 2018). Men suffering from abuse find it hard to know where to go.

Bed and breakfasts

Christa Maciver of charity Justlife reported, *"thousands of people are being forgotten in statistics with at least 51,500 in B&Bs as compared to 5,870 recorded by the government. There is so much we don't know and that we really need to be calculating homelessness more accurately....*

Their mental and physical health gets worse, and many can end up dead, but because they have a roof over their head – no matter how insecure – they are not counted within homelessness, when they should be. Only if we acknowledge the problem will we really be able to start finding solutions."

One B&B resident told of his experience of living in temporary accommodation for 18 months, saying,

"I'm totally depressed living there. You can't have anything nice. Things just go missing. You see, there aren't working locks on all

*the doors. In my room there are bare wires hanging out and I have
no light. I also feel vulnerable because anyone can get in or is let in
and it gets me down.*"[60]

Councils have advised that their use of B&Bs has almost tripled
over the past decade as accommodation options have narrowed.
They hear from parents who are at their wits end trying to raise
their children in one cramped room of a grotty B&B –
circumstances that no child should face. However, councils are
forced to pay out vast sums for emergency accommodation as
there is nowhere else to go, rather than being able to produce a
long-term home. According to Local Government Association, the
cost of B&Bs has risen from £10.6m in 2009-10 to £93.3m in
2017-8. Just think how the extra £82m could be put to better
use.[61]

Sofa surfing

A fifth of young people have sofa surfed in the past year and
almost half of them have done so for more than a month.[62]

Staying with friends was a more common situation than staying
with family. However, the average length of stay with a family
member was six months as compared to three months with a
friend. Almost half of those interviewed had been homeless for
more than two years, moving between different friends and
relatives.[63]

---

[60] Article 'More than 50,000 people homeless in B&Bs across UK – almost 10
times official figures', May Bulman, Social Affairs Correspondent of *The
Independent* edition of 24th April 2018 and the report by Christa Maciver of the
charity Justlife.
[61] Article 'B&B bill for homeless families soars', Chris Smyth, *The Times*, 12th
October 2019.
[62] Article 'A fifth of young people are homeless – you just can't see them', Paul
Noblet, *The Guardian*, 27th September 2017.
[63] Report 'Your Place, Not Mine', The Countryside Agency and Crisis,
November 2013.

Sofa surfing is a phenomenon that has largely grown unnoticed. By its very nature, sofa surfing goes on behind closed doors. In Britain, thousands of young people have no home and are moving from couch to couch just to keep themselves off the streets.

A number of young people were interviewed and described their experiences. Craig, 20, said *"It's hell, it's living hell. Sleeping rough is hell and in all fairness I don't think sofa surfing is much better."*

Alex was made homeless after a family breakdown when he was just 15. He describes the never-ending cycle of searching desperately for somewhere to stay, waking up and starting the whole process again.

Melissa, 21, who was alternating between staying with different friends and family, said, *"It messes with your head a lot. Your emotions and stuff like that, you might not show it, but it does affect you. If you've got nowhere to call home you're always uncomfortable, always unsettled, you're not safe, that's the key – safety."*[64]

Sam is on medication for depression and says that not having an address means he cannot register with a GP to get the mental health support he needs. *"It takes pretty much every day of my life, trying to find out where I am going to be staying. It doesn't feel like it ever ends. I feel quite drained with it all. I feel like I am going round in circles and circles and circles. All I can do is keep trying."*[65]

Nightstop and host schemes

Nightstop is an emergency housing provision in private homes whose residents have been carefully vetted and approved by

---

[64] Report 'The hidden homeless: Britain's young sofa surfer surge', Ciaran Jenkins, Channel 4 News, 4th December 2014.
[65] Report 'Sofa surfers: The young hidden homeless', BBC News, 21st December 2017.

homelessness agencies. The team react to a call from a young person who has just been made homeless, with a view to finding a host who will take in a HYP for a night.

That first night is often scary for the HYP and Nightstop avoids rough sleeping. The charity is then available to help find temporary accommodation and support the following day.

Recent research from DePaul UK , a large provider of Nightstop services, found host schemes caused the least harm to young people. The schemes, however, only offer limited support with issues such as welfare benefit claims, employment and training or finding long-term accommodation.[66]

Wider homelessness

As previously mentioned, wider homelessness includes staying with friends or relatives because the HYP is unable to find accommodation, has just been evicted, discharged from prison, hospital or other temporary accommodation without anywhere to stay, received a notice to quit and is unable to afford rent or a deposit, has been asked to leave by friends or relatives, or is in temporary accommodation.

Homeless charity properties

Having examined various forms of temporary homeless accommodation, I started looking at more permanent positions run by homeless charities. I sought out properties that appeared to be run as a home rather than an institution.

Some appeared to be a step up from a hostel but still had an institutional feel. Some were large properties with a permanent presence and the opportunity for HYP to access support services.

---

[66] Publication 'Danger zones and stepping stones, a qualitative exploration of young people's temporary living', Sarah McCoy, DePaul, 2018.

However, they still did not have the feel of a caring home that is structured to replace the family home and guide the HYP through to an independent life.

One such property could accommodate over 20 HYP, split into flats that contained three bedrooms, a kitchen and bathroom, with a communal lounge on the ground floor. However, the place was really dirty and felt cold. It seemed to me that the residents took no pride in the property. If residents take no responsibility for the property, they clearly do not regard it as a home and have no respect for the opportunity that they have been provided.

It may be easier to create a family home atmosphere with a smaller home, with up to seven residents, but I believe that much depends upon the quality of the charity's approach. Over the past 10 years, I have studied the way that one overseas charity has approached the problem.

Founded by a woman who was homeless in her youth, it helps over 1,000 HYP a year (some over a short period, dealing with specific issues such as family mediation, and others who stay for a longer period of time) and has a very high rate of success in helping HYP move to an independent life. Drug or alcohol is not tolerated and those who break the rules are referred on to rehabilitation clinics.

There are currently two homes, one of which has two buildings for living accommodation with capacity for around 50 residents in each. While there are a large number of residents, the atmosphere is very warm, largely due to the unique nature of the home and the quality of the support team onsite. Whenever I have visited, I have found the property to be very clean and felt inspired by the work they do and the reaction from the residents to their experience in the home.

The staff work with the residents to help them to develop their plan for the future. They must all adhere to the house rules, get up on time, breakfast and dine together, carry out their daily chores in the house and work towards their move on from the home as they establish independence. There is no fixed time for an onward move but most have progressed to an independent life within a couple of years.

Before looking at the number of properties required to house HYP, it is important to consider the type of property that is most suitable. There is no one size that fits all situations. In some cases, a small home with live-in support is appropriate. In other cases, larger properties could work, if the right support network is in place. The number of support staff to residents may depend upon the level and nature of support needs.

Private landlords

In the past, a large proportion of people at risk of homelessness would have their housing met by councils or housing associations. The Crisis report on private renting identified that many single homeless young people have no choice but to rent from a private landlord, particularly in England.

However, this option is often not fit for purpose because:

- The high up-front costs of deposits and rent in advance are a barrier;
- Many properties are in a poor condition and tenancy agreements do not offer long-term security;
- Rents are set at unaffordable levels.

We have seen how the misunderstanding and poor public perception of homelessness has a negative effect. Crisis research has found that landlords think, wrongly, that it is too risky to let their property to people claiming housing benefit.

In the Autumn 2017 Budget, the chancellor announced £20 million for Help to Rent projects to support homeless people, vulnerable tenants and landlords. The funding was designed to help fund services that match tenants with landlords and provide financial guarantees for deposits and rent, as well as ongoing support for both parties.

Crisis called on the government to do more to improve conditions for renters in England, including a change in the law (similar to the Canadian report I have mentioned) so that landlords have to be registered to rent and so make it easier for councils to tackle poor standards. They also called for longer term tenancies of at least three to five years and to limit rent increases during the tenancy.

There is clearly a need for a better working relationship with private landlords in terms of the perception of HYP and the way in which homeless charities and landlords interact. An article on 22nd November 2018 by Dionne for *The Big Issue* reported that landlords were attempting to launch a boycott of businesses that support the housing charity Shelter, according to housing industry website Property Industry Eye, which reported that while Shelter paid tribute to B&Q and Marks & Spencer for their support over the winter period, the National Landlords Alliance has targeted the stores.

According to the article, Doctor Ros Beck said that Shelter claims to get people into housing: *"Well, frankly, the only way they can do that is by persuading private landlords to take the risk of housing homeless people – as there is practically no social housing available for this purpose. In addition to allegedly helping people into housing we have also heard how they and others 'help' tenants remain in their housing by informing them that they can wait for the bailiffs in cases of eviction – a process that is ruinous and devastating for the landlords.*

You might think that given the fact that we are the only housing providers in a position to help with homelessness that they would build positive relationships with us in order to facilitate this. They do not do this, however. Instead they push a relentless anti private landlord agenda.'

Whatever the right and wrongs of this case, it is clear that a good working relationship with private landlords is important. Partnership working between social landlords and prevention services is essential.

The concerns of a social landlord are often quite simple; there is a need to ensure that rent is paid, that damage to housing is avoided and that community relationships are positive, both within social housing itself and between social tenants and any surrounding owner-occupiers and private rented sector tenants.

Both unfamiliarity in working with high-need people at risk of homelessness and the lack of an appropriate skillset can be a deterrent for social landlords and they may not have the resources to recruit specialist support staff themselves. If preventative and support services can offer guarantees that any housing management issues will be appropriately managed, this overcomes a potential barrier to social housing as a means of reducing homelessness.

Working with private landlords should involve ensuring that the housing they are providing is adequate and suitable for a potentially homeless person or household. Private sector landlords should be expected to maintain a basic quality standard and rent at a level that is affordable. This can be negotiated as part of a package that guarantees rent and provides housing management services.[67]

Move-on accommodation

A journey for a young person may involve going from the street to sofa surfing or other forms of temporary accommodation and

---

[67] Publication 'The Finnish Homelessness Strategy, An International review', Pleace N, Culhane D, Granfelt R and Knutagard M, 2015.

then to a home that is intended as a permanent residence for a year or two until that person is ready to move to independent living.

The problem at that time will be to find suitable accommodation at an affordable rate. A deposit will normally be required and the rent must be at a level that can be serviced out of earnings. There is a growing need for such affordable and available properties, especially in the major cities.

Housing backlog

The housing need in 2018 was reflected by the following:

- There was a backlog of housing need of 4.75 million households across the UK;
- Over 15 years, the total level of new housebuilding required is around 380,000 per year for Great Britain;
- Currently around 3.66 million households are in housing need;
- These figures include around 100,000 new social homes needed each year for the next 15 years (1,500,000 homes in total) with additional provision per year of 30,000 of shared ownership and 33,000 for intermediate rent across GB.[68]

The BBC News report of 21st November 2017 from the Reality Check team examined the projections. It stated that experts seem to agree on 300,000 a year as a good starting point but there is no universal confidence that this would make much difference to affordability.

---

[68] "Housing supply requirements across Great Britain: for low-income households and homeless people", Professor Glen Bramley, Heriot-Watt University for Crisis and the National Housing Federation, 2018.

Between April 2015 and the end of March 2017, a total of 287,600 homes were built, so if the government is going to meet its manifesto pledge from 2015 of a million homes by 2020, there needed to have been a considerable increase over the three years to 2020, to an average of more than 237,000 a year.

By recent standards, 300,000 is a very high number – the last time that many were completed in a year was in the financial year 1969-70. Christine Whitehead, professor of housing economics at LSE, questioned whether that many houses could be built. *"Would there be enough demand to make it worthwhile for suppliers to actually supply the housing? There are reasons why market completions have rarely exceeded around 170,000,"* she said.

Future developments

As society develops, the type of property needed changes. As communities move from one district to another, some properties are less well-attended. Religious centres, community centres and other buildings may fall into this category.

As high streets and industrial areas change, other buildings may become available. This can provide an opportunity for a charity to entice the landlord to sell or lease the building and so produce money for the landlord and a home for the homeless.

The World Population Review 2019 ranked countries by density of population. The UK ranked 49th out of 232 countries in terms of the highest density per square mile. In Europe, only the Netherlands and Belgium were more densely populated.

I do believe that one of the problems has been that as the population of the UK has risen, many have flocked to the cities, which have struggled to cope with the added pressure on the infrastructure.

As you travel around the UK by train, you will see huge swathes of land that could be used for residential accommodation. After World War II, garden cities were created as the country was rebuilt. This resulted in the building of houses, roads and other transport links on land and attracting business to those areas. Towns like Milton Keyes, Welwyn Garden City and Stevenage were created or extended. There has been some talk about using this approach as well as other means to free up land for development.

There may be some changes on the way to improve matters. 10 new towns have been promised by ministers hoping to kick-start post-Brexit regeneration and have been billed as Canary Wharfs of the north and Milton Keynes of the Midlands to bolster growth outside the south east of England. Ministers propose to change the law, if needed, to speed up the creation of new towns but will not be building on green belt land. It will be interesting to see how quickly they take effect.[69]

The urgency of the problem

We do need a long-term plan that will provide the right level of accommodation in a way that allows urban areas to operate effectively. In the short-term, we need significantly more of the right type of properties for the current homeless population.

If we do not rise to the challenge, cities in the UK could look more like San Francisco. Some years ago, my younger daughter returned from a trip to the US and had been shocked to see the number of homeless people in San Francisco. More recently, Emma Duncan visited her son in the city and painted a picture of what urban life could be like in her article 'The city of billionaires is a vision of hell' for *The Times*, October 2019.

---

[69] Article 'Ten new towns to bolster regions', Chris Smyth, *The Times*, 26th October 2019.

She regards San Francisco, a city with the highest density of billionaires on the planet, as the most visibly poor place she had visited outside India or South Africa. In that city, there are reported to be more than 8,000 homeless men and women on the streets, out of a population of less than 900,000. During her four-day trip, of the 10 shops she visited, homeless people walked into three, took items and walked out – the staff said that it happened seven or eight times a day. The police had apparently given up on property crime because it is so common and there is a certain sympathy for the perpetrators.

Those who have studied the problem say that the main explanation is the price of property where rents are about twice the London rate. The response has been rent controls but this has made the position worse as it discouraged people from letting out property and reduced supply; pushing up house prices further.

More homes are needed but the mayor has faced opposition. The right want to protect the value of their property and keep poor people at a safe distance. The left oppose development because it wants San Francisco to be the way it was in the 60s and distrusts property developers.

As reported, London is far from the hell that San Francisco has become but the number of homeless is visibly rising and unless we encourage more homebuilding, we could be heading in the same direction.

The current approach appears to be to look at the overall need for housing. However, there is a specific need for housing for the homeless. They do not appear to be treated as a special case that requires priority action. As part of an overall plan to combat youth homelessness, I would have thought that there should be a specific plan for this group, identifying the type of properties to be obtained for the different needs within this community.

This action should include housing to move HYP from the streets and temporary accommodation into appropriate homes and to cater for move-on accommodation. This could include gradually converting existing properties within the homeless sector (such as hostels) into a different form of housing.

Clearly urgent action is required to build new homes but other ideas should also be reviewed. The high street is changing, as technology has led to some companies having to rethink their business strategy. The conversion of shops and offices is one option but there could be industrial properties that have become outdated and could be used for HYP. Land will also have to be made available but it would be preferable for the government and local authorities to work with developers that have strong links to the homeless housing charities.

7

SERVICE PROVISION

Housing First

Having looked at the current accommodation provision and examined the services that are needed by HYP, we can now consider how the services are currently provided and then look at different approaches that may be used. Before doing so, it is as well to note a change that has generally been adopted with regard to the approach in the provision of help for HYP.

In some supported accommodation, a 'staircase model' is applied. This means that someone must engage with support services and demonstrate housing readiness before they can move to permanent accommodation. There is little evidence available on the extent to which this model is currently applied within the UK context.[70]

Housing First is a different approach. It was developed in the US by the organisation Pathways to Housing and is being delivered across the world. Housing First is the most important innovation in homelessness services design in the last few decades. It is proven to end homelessness for 80% of people with high support needs.

---

[70] Paper 'The Finnish Homeless Strategy: From a "Staircase" Model to a "Housing First" Approach to Tackling Long-Term Homelessness', Hannele Tainio and Peter Fredriksson.

The Housing First model prioritises rapid access to a stable home, from which other support needs are addressed through coordinated and intensive support. Permanent housing is provided without a test for housing readiness. Maintenance of the tenancy is not dependant on the tenant using support services. The model is specifically tailored for homeless people with complex needs. People can use a wide range of services to get personalised support when they need it and in their chosen format.

The success of the model depends on wider reforms, which clearly involve having access to stable and affordable housing, but it also depends on offering them a wide range of services which can offer timely personalised support in the format they choose. It needs to be part of an integrated strategy, to be truly effective. It is certainly appropriate for those with high and complex needs, while many would like to see it applied broadly across the homeless population.

The Housing First approach is seeking to get rid of temporary accommodation and place young people in a permanent home until they are ready to move on to independent living. The emphasis, particularly in Scotland, is to work on prevention first by having services such as family mediation and forms of early intervention. It is recognised that, with the best will in the world, family breakdown may still lead to homelessness, but the aim is to make the homeless period as short as possible.

One of the problems in the provision of services is the speed at which help can be obtained. For example, in countries such as Finland, social care services such as mental health support are provided almost immediately, whereas in some parts of the UK, it can take months to get the help needed; by which time the problems will have increased.

The other issue relating to Housing First is that resident selection may not be seen as a priority, although it can be an important issue in creating a home in which all the residents will feel comfortable.

Service provision research

While there is abundant research on service provisions, I found less information on the measurement of the quality of the delivery of services. As far back as 1999, research focused on access to services among HYP aged 14-25 in the Greater Manchester area and concluded that:

- Overall respondents found' particular difficulties in accessing help from statutory services, such as health;
- Significant numbers of HYP have had adverse experiences of institutions such as care services during childhood and adolescence – this may make them unwilling to make use of statutory and non-statutory services once homeless;
- Non-statutory services were widely used but many respondents revealed a lack of confidence in meeting some of their most basic needs and securing essential information;
- It appeared that the availability and quality of information did not match appropriately the needs of HYP. Often different agencies could make matters worse by providing conflicting information;
- The level of service provision was much greater in central Manchester than the surrounding towns;
- Reliable social networks can provide a source of information and advice as well as practical and emotional support;
- Elsewhere, studies of young, non-homeless people have shown significant associations between individuals' sense of community and subjective evaluations of wellbeing;[71]

---

[71] Paper 'Young homeless people and service provision', Paul Reid BAPG Dip and Hilary Klee BA Phd AFBPsS Cpsychol, 1999, (Downing-Orr, 1996), (Breakwell, 1986), Pretty et al. 1996.

Principles that were evidenced as key to successfully preventing youth homelessness included multi-agency working, a single point of access into services, a whole-family approach and positive professional relationships between staff and clients.[72]

Quality of advice

The trauma from living on the streets, having been rejected by your family or abused, may be the biggest issue that needs to be overcome. To open up to such a dreadful experience will normally require the obtaining of trust and patience.

We have seen that just getting a HYP into, say, a hostel is unlikely to solve the problem, as they can be chaotic in nature and not conducive to overcoming deep-lying problems. It will take another person off the streets and so improve the perception of the problem, but not advance matters alone.

Such is the need is for people in crisis that it is important to have available a high quality of service providers. As mental health problems can extend to depression, self-harm and even suicidal thoughts, the service needs to be appropriate. Timing of access can also be important. If a HYP is in a highly emotional state, it is essential that steps are put in place urgently to provide safety.

It is also important that the matter is treated with confidence and the approach taken is empathetic. There must be a belief that the service provider has the skills to help; especially if the quality of advice to date has been mixed.

Research from Mayday Trust

Mayday Trust talked to several hundred people and collated over 100 accounts in a series of blogs that they printed in a booklet

---

[72] Paper 'Preventing youth homelessness: what works?', Centrepoint.

called 'Wisdom from the Street' and their publication 'Homelessness system under construction'. They did not ask what people needed or why they had become homeless; rather, what they thought of homelessness services.

Two main themes came across from this work. Firstly, the current system and processes were not working for people who became homeless. The humanity and individuality of people's situations became lost. People's experience of the system reinforced helplessness, hopelessness and exclusion from community.

Secondly, the outcomes were not good enough. Too many people were either trapped in the system or moved on, only to return with a feeling of another failure under their belt.

The underlying principle of the Personal Transitions Service that they developed is that homelessness, leaving care, prison or psychiatric hospital is a brief transition in someone's life and with the right personalised intervention at the right time, people can achieve and sustain positive changes and independent living. While the research started in 2011, it is still relevant today. I have taken the following extracts from interviews conducted and conclusions reached to examine how service provision often fails the person in crisis.

We have seen that family breakdown and abuse is one of the most common reasons why young people find themselves homeless, but the way in which their trauma is handled often exacerbates the problem.

From what people told Mayday Trust, constant needs and risk assessments made them feel humiliated at best, re-traumatised at worst: *"I was abused by my step-dad. I drink a litre of vodka a day. I had unprotected sex last week. Now your turn... I didn't think so."*

Having to tell often painful stories, over and over again, was distressing. Disclosing very personal information to people they did not know made the homeless people become distant from themselves, or they 'became their problem' and adopted it as their identity. Eventually, this approach was institutionalising people to the point where they felt they had no hope of a better life or being defined as anything other than the combination of their needs.

Getting behind the reasons for substance abuse was essential, but too often the aim was to find out what the problems were and then set about trying to fix them, without understanding that people were not ready to give up the things that were helping them cope. *"What I need isn't just to come off drugs, quit alcohol and to get a job. I need to feel I'm worth something, then I might want to do those things."*

Many used drugs, alcohol or self-harming as ways to cope with traumatic experiences. Some did so to keep in with their friends and forget about their situation. Without finding more positive things to replace them, they needed something to get them through the night.

The misery of living in poor forms of temporary accommodation was illustrated by the research: *"That's just what I need. More pills and someone to talk to about why I feel crazy. You would too if you slept in a tiny room next to someone screaming all night."*

Significant numbers of people talked of being prescribed drugs for depression, anxiety or bipolar disorders, when in reality, their emotional distress was related to homelessness, isolation and abuse from people around them. Suicidal thoughts or attempts were often a result of events in the past or their circumstances – for example, living in unsuitable housing where they were intimidated or did not feel safe. *"Yeah we're a great community at my hostel. I'm perfectly safe here (as long as I hand over my money to my roommate and don't let anyone else know.)"*

People who had spent longer periods in hostels talked about being controlled by others who lived there. This included financial abuse and an unhealthy dependency on drugs and alcohol as a way of joining in with the social scene and, ultimately, staying safe. For many, their plight was one of stagnation rather than progression. *"Because most of the hostels in Oxford, you stay about a year and then if you haven't been kicked out then they usually try and move you on. But the thing is, the only place to move on is to one of the other hostels... And that's all you do. You just keep bouncing backwards and bounce and bounce about and it was, it's just to keep the sub-culture going... The support structure there to help us is the one that puts all the obstacles up..."*

Most people talked about unrealistic rules which worked against their ability to get out of their situation, including not always having access to their belongings or passports. In some accounts, people had clearly become institutionalised in their accommodation, where meals were provided for them and people had very little power and control over day to day living.

Interventions were not always relevant to what people needed and wanted. They ended up attending key working sessions that were more focused on ticking boxes, rather than addressing what was really going on in their lives. The interventions were not 'real world'. Having to engage in activities that didn't reflect their interests, spending months on waiting lists and undertaking courses to prove that they were ready to move out of the homelessness sector was often further proof of how far they had fallen in life.

Rather than focus on the negatives, the research suggested that people are more likely to take responsibility for their own lives and make the change that matters to them if they have opportunities that build on their strengths. Likewise, individuals who feel their strengths and abilities are recognised by others are able to develop the necessary grit to bounce back from tough life experiences and sustain positive change in the long term.

"It's the positive way they work with you instead of focusing on the bad aspects. They come at it from the other side. And coming at it from the other side of the fence, it's a bit alien but it works because when you start doing things that you're interested in, that you enjoy, that you've got passion for, you wake up and you feel better. You've got a purpose, you've got something. It gives you that motivation, that drive again..."

Based upon the research gathered, the model created by the Mayday Trust focused on building an individual's assets as a means for them to take control of their lives and make the positive changes they wanted for themselves.

This differed from the traditional support, which relies on needs and risks assessment to set goals usually defined around a narrow grouping of areas, such as maintaining tenancy, reducing substance misuse, offending behaviour, improving physical and mental health or mediating family relationships.

As part of the process of taking control, it is important to have access to opportunities in the local community, such as volunteering centres, colleges for training and education, social groups, art centres, music studios and sports clubs, where people can engage in their interests and hobbies.

Challenging existing traditional practices and processes that have often been the norm for many years can be extremely difficult, especially as austerity has created highly competitive and unstable environments. However, it is only by creating the right environment for young people in crisis to thrive that positive outcomes can be achieved.

As previously mentioned, the mix of residents is important to both ensure that individuals will not be subject to negative influences that could worsen their position and that they have a positive social support network.

Breadth of advice

If we revert to the range of support needs, they included different mental or physical health problems, drug or alcohol abuse, domestic and sexual abuse, criminality and anti-social behaviour, further education, employment, benefits assistance and life skills development. This is not a comprehensive list but it is wide enough to realise that there is a requirement to have a broad range of available experts and that first, trust between the HYP and a key worker must be won.

Who is the key provider of services?

Many HYP are having to fend for themselves, once they have obtained accommodation, with a view to getting the help required. I believe that the best approach is to have a well-trained, empathetic support worker as the key contact but for that person to be within an organisation where the main support services are available in-house, yet referral to external experts is available as required.

I initially see the most important person to be that support worker (who I now refer to as the 'key worker') who needs to develop a relationship of trust and respect with the HYP over time to ensure that the appropriate support services are being provided and that they are succeeding. This will require ongoing monitoring and further action as required, as well as help from the other staff within the charity (whom I will now refer to as 'support workers'). The key worker may link with a line manager or service consultants within the organisation, so the support workers are not subordinate to the key worker; rather a different form of employee within the homeless charity.

In my professional life I worked for a firm that developed an approach whereby the client would have one partner who was responsible for all aspects of the services required by the client. Specialist partners would be brought in to provide specific expertise but the general partner would be fully aware of the case throughout. This approach generally worked very well, as the client developed a sound, long-term relationship with one person and had the benefit of access to experts. Of course, the success of the relationship always depended upon providing high-quality advice and communicating well.

These principles can easily apply to HYP, where the main, ongoing relationship is with the key worker, who is a constant source of support until the young person has made the transition to independence. Even then, the two may well stay in touch to maintain the success achieved.

Whether to keep the advice in-house or seek external support is also an important matter, relevant whether you are running a professional practice or a homeless charity. I was always impressed by my doctor, who seemed to know exactly when to refer a patient to a consultant rather than try to treat the illness himself. It was an important skill.

The key worker tends to set the tone in the house, with the aim of making it warm and inclusive, but with rules that the residents must buy into from the outset and keep to throughout.

Recruitment and retention

Many large professional firms and commercial businesses have a requirement to take in a large number of school leavers and graduates to fill the next year's intake and so ensure that the businesses continue to grow and meet the demands of their clients and customers. Some attend universities to pitch for the best graduates.

While fundraising is an important element of any plan, success is only achieved with the right people. If we are to plan to reduce youth homelessness, we will need the right key workers and support workers, and we must consider how best to attract those people. This could be by recruiting those with some of the support skills needed and training them to cover the gaps in their experience. However, it would be better to train the right people from the outset. That may mean designing specific courses at colleges and university and seeking to identify potential candidates at school before they leave.

Having recruited the right people, there is then the issue of retention. Employees starting a career want to develop and take on new challenges. Those who may be asked to deliver their services by living with the HYP may not wish to do so for ever and, over time, may want to live in their own home. Therefore, only certain people may be happy to 'live at work' and they will need to have their own space and separate accommodation.

It may be that if you had a steady stream of candidates who were happy to live with HYP for a number of years, they could train up the next generation of key workers when they move on within the homeless charity network. The next generation of key workers could also come from a HYP background themselves who have achieved independence or are ready to move on. Who better to understand the issues faced by homelessness than someone who has had first-hand experience?

8

OUTREACH

Training

By identifying the core and hidden homeless population, we can put the right measures in place, identify the true scale of the problem, raise awareness of what is required and monitor the individual cases, positive outcomes, issues arising and level of youth homelessness in the UK.

Before looking at the various outreach approaches to the different forms of homelessness, it is worth considering the work of the outreach worker. This was illustrated in an article in *The Guardian* on 15th February 2016 entitled, 'The secret life of a homeless outreach worker: we put up with abuse that no other professional would'.

The anonymous outreach worker for a well-known homeless charity recorded, *"If I meet someone new and tell them about it, you can guarantee they will say "That must be rewarding." And it can be, sometimes. But just as often it is frustrating, bewildering, exhausting, tedious and not a suitable line of work if you have a poor circulation or a delicate sense of smell... The most vulnerable people rely on us, but we are rarely qualified in the specialisms they desperately need. We are usually not mental health professionals, addiction experts or psychotherapists – or rather we don't have those certificates. Experience, empathy and common sense are good substitutes up to a point..."*

An outreach worker at The Connection, St Martin-in-the Fields, gave an illustration of a 25-year-old woman from Liverpool who had been seen sleeping rough. The young woman did not want to disclose much information, but the worker was determined to keep returning to talk to her and to establish what had happened in order to encourage her into some temporary housing, however long this might take.

These outreach workers tend to seek out those who can be found on the streets or have been referred rather than the hidden homeless, such as sofa surfers. However, a national strategy should include an examination of the appropriate level of training to make their lives easier and more effective, as they are often the first point of contact in trying to get a homeless person the help needed.

Walking the street

I was interested to understand a little more about the work of an outreach team, so joined them on their night-time trawl of the area that they cover in and around a London borough.

They were aware of the large number of HYP in their patch and so part of the reason for walking the streets was to find those they had arranged to meet and whom were known to them, as well as identifying any new HYP who were sleeping rough.

London can be a very different place at night. The outreach workers had great knowledge of the characters on the streets. They pointed out the drug dealing that I would not have noticed and knew how to handle any potentially difficult situations.

I mentioned a young person I had spotted earlier, coming into the centre, but who was nowhere to be seen, and they immediately knew who I meant and that person's background.

They had clearly developed a good relationship with those we met and knew what they needed to do to progress. It seemed to me a thankless task that was carried out with professionalism and empathy. By its very nature, though, it is rather hit and miss, as it depends upon who is found at the time. Regardless, it does provide a very valuable service.

Street homelessness

There are a number of charities with an outreach team that will go out at night to cover their catchment area with a view to identifying HYP sleeping rough, trying to get them into any available temporary accommodation and encouraging them to call into their drop-in centre for help of a long-term nature.

There are not enough outreach workers to cover all of the UK and some rough sleepers will not be easily found. Those sleeping in doorways are out in the open, but others may be hiding in any manner of places, away from view.

Some HYP may feel that there is little point in approaching a local authority but if there was greater confidence in a starting point of contact, that would lead to an acceptable solution to their problems and perhaps there would be a greater number of those young people making contact. There are no easy answers but as the UK improves its services to the HYP population and finds ways to better publicise its approach, services and points of contact, the number of rough sleepers may start to fall.

Public transport

The number of people sleeping on night buses or trains is on the rise. However, there are systems in place to report these people and the charities helping HYP should be able to ensure that any in their area are identified and helped.

Squats

The relevant charities would normally be in touch with the police and other services to identify any HYP in squats that should be better served in permanent accommodation as the properties become available.

Hostels, refugees, winter shelters and B&Bs

As permanent accommodation becomes available, a concerted effort can be made to contact the numerous hostels and winter shelters around the country and encourage any HYP to meet with the relevant local charity so that they can be placed in homes that are suitable; taking account of their particular circumstances and needs.

Identifying the HYP in a bed and breakfast may be more difficult unless systems are in place to keep a central register of all people in temporary accommodation.

Nightstop

The Nightstop system is operated by homeless charities such as DePaul and HYP can be moved into permanent accommodation as it becomes available.

Sofa surfing

This is perhaps the most difficult group of people to identify as they are truly hidden from view and comprise a high proportion of the HYP population. Many stay with friends or family for a short while, for various reasons, such as family breakdown. It is normally difficult for them to progress in these circumstances and they clearly need to find permanent accommodation. What sometimes starts off as a helping hand from a friend can become very stressful for the homeless person, as well as the friend or family. Young people may decide not to seek help from a local authority for various reasons and so are not known to any organisation that can help.

Some of the ways to reach HYP sofa surfers include contact with:

- Schools;
- Colleges;
- Communities – churches, mosques, temples etc.;
- Social media platforms;
- Bloggers.

Sixth form teachers often have a good idea as to the background situation of their pupils and can identify cases where a young person would be better served in a permanent home to complete studies and seek employment; often away from a chaotic existence at home or sofa surfing. In particular, teachers working in schools in deprived areas can be a good source of referrals. Likewise, college tutors can be another source but may not have known the young person as well, or for a long period of time.

Case workers

Developing trust is essential so that a young person in crisis feels comfortable talking about difficult issues and can start to open up about the past and how to look to a brighter future. An institutionalised approach can not only stifle progress but make it harder for the young person to try again to plan for the future.

Some organisations are swamped with too many cases and lack funds to provide the right level of resources, leaving a HYP who does make contact with insufficient time for the session. The regularity of meetings may also be too sporadic to really make a difference.

The Mayday Trust research showed that some people were initially positive about 'key working' sessions and many valued the relationship with their key worker, including the practical help and advice they received on issues such as welfare benefits.

However, a significant number of people said they only attended weekly sessions to comply with their plan so that they would be nominated for accommodation. Many expressed unhappiness at turning up every week in small institutional offices just to talk about their 'issues'. They disliked being constantly reminded about their situation and having to talk about their problems at a time and place that was often dictated to them. It was draining and it did not inspire them to want to turn up. Many sessions left them feeling worse about themselves rather than engaged and motivated.[73]

A national awareness

It is essential for there to be a much more comprehensive understanding of the hidden homeless community. The difficulty is in knowing exactly how to reach out to young people in crisis or those who know of their plight. It is also important not to create undeliverable expectations.

A good start is the Centrepoint homeless databank, which collects information from government and local authority sources. It relies upon people presenting themselves to a local authority, but many HYP do not do so, for various reasons. Some feel that they will get nowhere while others may not know what to do or may think that their situation is temporary but later find that their homelessness persists.

A campaign to identify the hidden homeless who have not presented themselves to a local authority and are not on the Centrepoint databank would help to provide a better understanding of the scale of the problem. Information can then be provided as to where help may be available. It would also identify the additional resources needed within the youth homeless sector to provide the right level of support required.

---

[73] Research 'Wisdom from the street', Mayday Trust.

It is possible to reach out to young people through local communities but the results can be inconsistent. Many HYP have a phone and are in touch with their friends, even if not their family. Reaching out through the right social media platforms can also produce a good response. However, there will need to be a team of social media savvy people involved to make this work.

Bloggers and celebrities get huge numbers of followers these days. They could also play a part in reaching out to identify where help can be found.

There are no easy answers and a lot of hard graft will be needed to firstly identify sofa surfers and then ensure that they get the help they need. Reaching out too early, before help is in place, can be counter-productive, so a coordinated approach is required.

Referrals

When I made contact with various people in my local community to discuss youth homelessness, I was interested to learn that many of those who may become aware of young people in crisis had little idea where to turn when they wanted to help and refer on that person. Four cases were highlighted in the space of a few weeks.

An assistant head of a local school called, as he was trying to help a sixth former who was shortly to be taking A levels and had suddenly found himself homeless. The local authority was one option but they appeared to be understaffed and were not reacting as fast as he wanted.

A charity did have accommodation, but no wrap-around services, and it was clear that this HYP was likely to need professional counselling while other charities were available to help. The problem appeared to be one where an earlier intervention may have helped, but those discussions were not normally available. When the problem surfaced, there appeared to be a panic to avoid the issue worsening at this critical time. If a solution could be found and the HYP could gain some stability and get the required grades, the university should be able to solve the accommodation issue.

Another case related to a young woman in an abusive relationship needing a speedy exit, accommodation and support services. Again, the charity helping her seemed at a loss regarding what to do.

A third case related to a young man who had been abused and needed help. Again, the person he turned to was not aware of how to solve the problem, nor the best referral option.

A fourth case related to a young person who was estranged from her mother, looking after her younger sister, and in a state of crisis. Her friend wanted to get her help but did not know where to turn and was referred on to a relevant charity.

There did not appear to be a community solution, so those coming into contact with young people in crisis did not know how to respond. In some cases, it was a lack of understanding of the potential referral options, in other cases, there were no effective options, and in all cases, the issues had been developing for some time.

Recently, a debate has been raging about who is responsible for gang warfare and knife crime in the UK. Comments have been made about schools, police, medical and nursing professionals needing to take a more active involvement in notifying problem cases, and this could be extended to notifying cases of young people in crisis that may lead to homelessness. The professions responded by stressing the lack of resources to do their basic job, let alone being able to deal with these social problems, and that the responsibility starts with the parents.

I have seen how dedicated teachers can be when identifying an issue. In the aforementioned case, the assistant head was going well beyond his expected duties and spending considerable time trying to find a solution, without getting much help in the process. We do need to consider how there can be a better, joined-up approach between initially identifying a potential problem and having the necessary referral options available.

Coordination

Overall, it seems to me as though outreach is rather hit and miss, at present. This may partly be because of the nature of the work. The dedicated efforts of outreach staff to walk the street, seeking out young people in crisis, is to be commended so that these young people can then be encouraged to come into the drop-in centre for a more structured assessment and ongoing help.

I feel that more thought is needed as to how to engage with young people in crisis at an earlier time. Most have access to a phone and perhaps part of the way forward is the development of more tools that can be accessed in this way. There seems to be little incentive for young people in crisis to reach out for help, and often a lack of knowledge on how to do so.

PART III

THE PARTIES INVOLVED

"Looking at the impact philanthropy has already had, if everyone gets involved we can do something that's never been done before."

Source: extract from a talk by Bill Gates at the National Museum of American History, Washington DC, 1st December 2015.

9

HOMELESS CHARITIES

UK national homeless charities

There are many charities helping to fight homelessness, ranging from large national charities that may be well-known to the public, to small local charities. Some provide a wide range of services whereas others help with particular aspects of homelessness.

Charities working at a local and national level to fight homelessness include Crisis, Shelter, The Big Issue Foundation, Centrepoint, Depaul UK, St Mungo's, Emmaus UK, Homeless Link and Streetlink.

From my experience in liaising with these charities, all have a slightly different approach and some cover different areas of specialisation. For example, Crisis has created great awareness of the plight of the homeless through their excellent research papers and Crisis at Christmas.

Shelter offers advice, information, representation and advocacy to people who are homeless, in unsuitable or insecure housing, or at risk of becoming homeless, via online support networks as well as advice and support services.

Depaul UK is a global network whose work ranges from providing safe shelter, accommodation, food and health services to helping people affected by homelessness receive education, employment and the social services they need. It provides support for HYP, offering emergency accommodation and longer-term housing, as well as outreach services to help young people in crisis.

The Big Issue Foundation was founded to offer outreach to vendors. Their work includes helping vendors get to housing meetings or job interviews, open bank accounts, get passports, access health care, receive training and education and make the move from the street to a hostel, from a hostel to temporary accommodation or on to something more permanent, before helping out with the essentials to set up home. The sale of *The Big Issue* magazine by vendors helps homeless people start the process of getting back into work. The vendors tend to structure their lives to earn money as a pathway to independence.

Centrepoint supports more than 9,200 HYP in the 16-24 age group in London, Manchester, Yorkshire and the north east of England. It also provides more than 1,000 bed spaces for young people from the 60 accommodation centres it runs in Sunderland, Bradford, Manchester, Barnsley and 14 boroughs in London.

St Mungo's is a large charity that provides outreach, support and shelter for homeless people and has services across the south of England working to help people rebuild their lives. Like Crisis, it seeks to improve understanding of homelessness and empathy towards homeless people.

Emmaus UK has a slightly different approach. Like The Big Issue Foundation, it supports people out of homelessness, providing meaningful work as well as housing in a community setting. Through social enterprises, it raises funds for food, accommodation and a small living allowance for its 'companions'. The work includes refurbishing and selling donated furniture and household goods in their shops and showrooms, running cafes, house clearance businesses and gardening projects.

Homeless Link works with other charities and organisations to try to improve services while also working with local and national government to improve policies.

Streetlink connects rough sleepers to homeless services. It runs a website, app and phoneline enabling members of the public to report rough sleepers in England and Wales – the information is then passed on to the local authority outreach teams, who will attempt to contact the individual and connect them with vital services.

New Horizon Youth Centre ("NHYC")

Each year, thousands of young people across London become homeless because of family breakdown, domestic abuse, poverty, gang violence, or war and persecution in their home country.

Under-resourced local authorities are only able to help a limited number of the most extreme cases, so the rest end up homeless and vulnerable at a critical point in their young lives. They try to hold on to college places and take minimal wage jobs (35% of the clients of NHYC are in work or education while homeless) but do not earn enough to cover the spiralling cost of private rents. Their struggle to build a better life is often lost in the battle to find somewhere to sleep.

NHYC is a vital support network for 16-24-year-olds who have nowhere else to turn. At its drop-in centre, NHYC provides everything from hot food, showers and laundry to finding accommodation, training and employment for HYP. It offers counselling, drug and alcohol support, health, fitness, art, music and communication skills workshops – everything they need to create a positive future.

NHYC supports around 2,500 16-24-year-olds every year; the majority of whom are in urgent need of housing. NHYC helps its clients with accommodation by:

- Making referrals into hostels, shelters and other accommodation;
- Helping with benefit problems or making claims;
- Advising with appeals for those who have been sanctioned;
- Helping in communicating with probation, police, social workers or hostel workers;
- Finding support for those with debt problems;
- Finding support for those who may be homeless due to a relationship breakdown;
- Getting legal advice from a solicitor;
- Keeping an emergency fund to cover urgent accommodation needs.

NHYC helps its clients prepare for the workplace. Its dedicated team support young people who are not in education, employment or training by:

- Providing assistance with job search and job applications, interviews, presentations and CV-writing skills;
- Finding work placements, apprenticeships or volunteering opportunities;
- Helping with college applications, UCAS applications, help with various paperwork and advice;
- Working towards positive futures through goal setting and one-to-one coaching;
- Providing weekend learning programmes for homeless young people;
- Supporting and encouraging schemes such as the Social Enterprise Project.

NHYC runs a range of life skills workshops and also operates a weekend service that provides additional support such as ESOL classes for students with English as their second language. Its Health Team covers a range of activities on all aspects of physical and emotional health. Its Youth Outreach Project works with vulnerable young people on the streets and in prison.

It also delivers workshops on subjects such as sexual exploitation, running away from home and homelessness prevention across London via youth clubs, schools and other places where young people congregate.

Outside London

While a large proportion of HYP are in London, what about those outside of the capital? Apart from the national charities such as Centrepoint and Shelter, there are numerous charities for HYP. To mention just a few, St Basils operates in Birmingham, Barnabus in Manchester, Rock Trust in Scotland, Llamau in Wales and MACS in Northern Ireland. Some of the larger regional charities provide housing with floating support, whereas some provide in-house support.

For example, Llamau supports the most vulnerable young people and women in Wales. They are particularly well-known for working with those most at risk; care leavers, those who have been involved with the criminal justice system, people who have experienced domestic abuse and those who have had chaotic and disadvantaged lifestyles. They provide high levels of individual support to help them gain the skills necessary to live independent and purposeful lives in their communities.

The Clock Tower Sanctuary in Brighton operates a drop-in day centre for young people in crisis and has plans to expand its services. Interestingly, the homeless situation in Brighton is a little different from London and some other major cities, as there appear to be more young people sleeping rough in Brighton as a proportion of the total population of HYP, whereas in London, there currently appear to be proportionately more hidden homeless. However, in other respects, there are similarities, in that accommodation in Brighton is relatively expensive, at a similar level to London.

Catch 22

While NHYC operates a day centre and has specialists to provide the support services, other charitable and social provision operates by outsourcing these services. For example, Catch 22 is a national charity that delivers services by contract to institutions such as local authorities, schools and prisons. They can also provide services for care leavers and other young people who may otherwise be homeless.

Different communities

LGBT Jigsaw is a partnership between Stonewall Housing, Galop, The Albert Kennedy Trust and Pace. These four organisations have varying expertise in working with lesbian, gay, bisexual and transgender young people. They also work with those who are questioning their sexuality or gender identity. These people can find themselves homeless following abandonment by their family and need help to live an independent life.

There are certain charities that cater for a particular group. For example, The Haven in Wolverhampton supports women and dependent children who are vulnerable to domestic violence, homelessness and abuse.

Different ethnic groups have come together to help the homeless. As reported in 2016: *"Muslims are handing out sleeping kits in London, Sikhs and Hindus are housing homeless people in Leicester, and Jews are feeding them in St Albans."* The article went on to say that Anglicans, Catholics, Methodists, Quakers, Jews, Hindus, Muslims and Sikhs opened a night shelter in Leicester in what was believed to be the first enterprise of its kind.[74]

Salma Ravat of One Roof had an interesting take on a side benefit of multi-ethnic cooperation: *"It's really important that all these*

---

[74] Article 'Muslims and Christian groups working together to help the homeless at Christmas', Peter Walker, *The Independent*, 22nd December 2016.

different faiths work together. It builds community: people getting to know each other, sharing values and sharing morals. Working together, you find out more about what you have in common with one another than what your differences are."

Onside

There are so many UK charities that are either directly involved in youth homelessness or have a link to the social issues faced by young people. Onside Youth Zones is an inspirational charity that has sought to tackle the problems that young people face in deprived areas. Too often there is nothing for them to do outside of school hours and this feeds into recruitment into gangs leading to crime, drugs and a violent environment.

Onside's aim has been to create a safe space for young people aged eight to 19 (up to 25 if disabled) to gather in their leisure time. The activities at the youth zones include dance, arts and crafts, sport, and games. It has a counselling service and provides an opportunity for positive social interaction and learning new skills. It also helps to break down barriers, reach isolated young people and foster cohesion within the community in an inter-faith approach.

The construction of each new youth zone is a four-way link between the private sector funding, local authority, young people and the community. More than 38,000 members make around 500,000 visits to Onside Zones which are located around the UK in the most disadvantaged communities.

Landaid

Landaid comes at the homelessness issue from the property perspective. Inspired by Bob Geldof's Live Aid, Landaid was formed in 1986 to bring together the property industry to reduce youth homelessness. They now give grants of up to £2 million a year, largely focused on building work projects for living accommodation. Between 2017 and February 2019, they were able to create more than 470 bed spaces. They also arrange for skilled property professionals to give free property advice to UK charities.

Their strategic partners are companies who annually donate over £30,000 to Landaid and have made a long-term strategic commitment to solve youth homelessness. When searching for suitable properties for young people in crisis, there will often be the need to make some structural changes to conform to various legislation and to acquire and retain a licence for a house with multiple occupancy or to the requirements of a local authority provider. Landaid could provide the necessary finance to turn an opportunity into reality. The charity can also refer on property advisers who are prepared to give advice pro bono to homeless charities.

Financial institutions

There are a number of organisations that are a source of financial support for homeless charities. For example, Nationwide Building Society awards grants and social investments through the Nationwide Foundation which tackle the root causes of the social issues that lead to disadvantage, poverty and inequality.

The Lloyds Bank Foundation is another charity that partners with small and local charities to help people overcome complex social issues such as mental health, homelessness and domestic abuse. Their size and understanding of the people and local communities they work with means they are able to make life-changing impact where others cannot. These charities are under-funded, under pressure and too often ignored.

Collaboration

Back in 2000, Alison Benjamin of *The Guardian* questioned whether there were too many charities.[75] At the time, there were

---

[75] Article 'Too many cooks?', Alison Benjamin, *The Guardian*, 8th November 2000.

185,000 registered charities in England and Wales, including 650 cancer charities and more than 200 charities working with homeless people, just in London. With 5,000 new charities created every year, a poll at the time reflected the rise in public scepticism. It showed that 70% of the public thought that there were too many charities doing similar work and competing with each other.

Different views were expressed. Gordon McVie, director general of Cancer Research Campaign, felt that it would be inappropriate for the four big cancer charities to merge. He said that they jointly fund research projects, that research suggested that they raise more money separately and that volunteers and donors are loyal to a brand.

Charities expert Moira Guthrie warned that mergers are no panacea – they eat up time and money in the short term, services can suffer and they are not a guarantee to success. If attention is concentrated on the vision for the future services and how to achieve it, the potential strategic value of partnership becomes clear. That reflects the creation of The London Youth Gateway partnership. It is also essential that the homeless charities link with other specialist organisations.

The Prince's Trust is a wonderful initiative created by the Prince of Wales and I am aware of its great work and how charities have used its services as well as its link with homeless-friendly companies. The next generation of royalty is also taking an active interest in reducing youth homelessness, as the Duke and Duchess of Cambridge and Prince Harry recently signalled that they intend their respective charity work to focus on bringing organisations together under key themes, including mental health, veterans, homelessness, wildlife and cyberbullying.

However, Prince William said, *"I do wonder at times if the compassion which leads people to set up or maintain charities could not be equally well directed at first finding opportunities to work with existing charities.*

Competition for funds between an ever-growing number of charities, and the confusion it can cause among donors, can lead to the silo-ing of expertise and, at worst, territorial behaviour. I know that this message is not always easy to hear: Charities exist because those who work and volunteer for them each believe passionately in its importance and they are right to do so.

But as the challenges of the future begin to bear down on us, I believe that the big shift must begin to happen – the sector must be open to collaborate, to share expertise and resources; to focus less on individual interests and more on the benefits that working together will bring. That, I believe, is where the future lies."[76]

From my personal liaison with various homeless charities, both large and small, I feel that they do differ in terms of approach and flexibility. That is no bad thing, as a donor can select the charity of choice and, when it comes to larger donations, may have a possibility of getting involved within proper compliance boundaries.

These charities need to link with numerous organisations including local authorities, providers of accommodation (such as landlords), specialists regarding the service provisions (such as mental health experts), prisons, places of further education, employers, benefit departments etc.

Perhaps one form of collaboration could be the production of an action plan for the reduction of youth homelessness (as well as a plan that covers the homeless of all ages), setting out the roles of each charity and the manner in which the initiative can be resourced. This could be particularly important if major donors can be found who would be prepared to provide significant funding on the condition that such a plan can be developed.

---

[76] Article 'Charities must work together or risk confusing donors, Prince Williams warns', Hannah Furness, *The Telegraph*, 23rd January 2018.

10

THE STATE

The role of the state

Many people have grappled with the role of the state in society and its interplay with the private sector and so it is as well to consider its mandate. The role of the state is said to include the maintenance of industrial peace, order, and safety, the protection of persons and property, and the preservation of external security.

From a more pragmatic view, it provides the function of organising and managing structural relations within society; the function of creating political, legal and economic conditions to encourage the development of individual spheres in the life of society and the function of ensuring respect for the law and combating organised crime and corruption.

It consists of the government or legislature which passes the laws, the bureaucracy or civil service, which implements the governmental decisions and the national security forces, such as the police and army, which enforce the law and protect the state from threats respectively. Some political scientists believe that the state can also consist of health and welfare services and education.[77]

The economist Martin Wolf considered how far the protective role of the state should go: *"In the 1970s, the view that democracy would collapse under the weight of its excessive promises seemed*

---

[77] Gerth and Mills, 1948.

to me disturbingly true. I am no longer convinced of this... More-over, the capacity for learning by democracies is greater than I had realised. The conservative movements of the 1980s were part of that learning.

But they went too far in their confidence in market arrangements and their indifference to the social and political consequences of inequality. I would support state pensions, state-funded health insurance and state regulation of environmental and other externalities...

The ancient Athenians called someone who had a purely private life 'idiotes'. This is, of course, the origin of our word 'idiot'. Individual liberty does indeed matter. But it is not the only thing that matters. The market is a remarkable social institution. But it is far from perfect. Democratic politics can be destructive. But it is much better than the alternatives. Each of us has an obligation, as a citizen, to make politics work as well as he (or she) can and to embrace the debate over a wide range of difficult choices that this entails."

You could argue that the state alone has the responsibility to cure homelessness, but I would suggest that this is wildly optimistic in the current climate. I believe that while the state has an important role to play, it should be part of the solution.

The link between what should be done by the state, the private sector and each individual within society is likely to continue to be debated but what is clear is that all relevant parties will be needed to help bring youth homelessness under control.

Wealth creation

Anand Giridharadas' recent *New York Times* bestseller 'Winner Takes All: The elite charade of changing the world' provided a very interesting insight into the way in which the ultra-wealthy have accumulated wealth before becoming philanthropists.

It examined how, before becoming philanthropists, some ultra-wealthy may have created problems that they are now seeking to solve through charity work. For example, owners of food companies that have contributed to diabetes through food and drink with a high sugar content, or companies that have treated staff poorly without providing job security may have contributed to poverty and homelessness.

I appreciate that we need to look carefully at how businesses make their profit, but that is beyond the scope of this book. My starting point is to consider how best to source the money needed to make a significant impact in reducing youth homelessness from the wealth that has accumulated to date.

Also, I do believe that we must encourage wealth creation so as to give us the best opportunity to encourage those with 'surplus funds' to use that money for charitable works. Poor economies usually lead to greater poverty. You only have to look at the way that Venezuela's economy has been run – a country that has had more oil than Saudi Arabia but could not feed its people.

Personal asset values

It is important that steps are taken to redress the imbalance in our society. Inequality has widened of late, with the world's richest 1% now owning half the world's wealth. At the other end of the spectrum, the world's 3.5 billion poorest adults each have assets of less than £7,600. The number of millionaires increased by 170% between 2000 and 2017, while the number of ultra-high net worth individuals rose five-fold.

At the time of writing, it appears to be the new technology-based industries that have created huge wealth, with the top 10 wealthiest people including Bill Gates (Microsoft), Mark Zuckerberg (Facebook), Jeff Bezos (Amazon), Larry Ellison (Oracle), Carlos Slim (Telemex) and Michael Bloomberg (computer finance terminals).

In the UK, the wealthiest 1% have seen their share increase to nearly a quarter of all the county's wealth. Concern has also been expressed that tax avoidance is preventing money being used to tackle poverty in the UK and overseas.

The biggest losers are young people, who do not expect to become as rich as their parents. While millennials are much more educated than their parents, it is expected that only a minority of high achievers and those in demand sectors, such as technology or finance, can expect to overcome the 'millennial disadvantage'.

The political class

We appear to be the most divided, in-debt, obese, addicted generation in recent times. There has been a collapse in respect for politicians and what they can achieve. The expenses scandal led to a feeling that they were dishonest over their remuneration, although we need to ask ourselves whether they are paid appropriately or trained for the job. They often do not stay in the job long enough to have a chance to fully understand the issues of their department, let alone implement them. However, these are the people we expect to tackle complex social problems.

There also needs to be honesty about the current state of affairs, what can be achieved and what is being achieved under their watch. The public have become tired of the political blame game and the production of targets that have little chance of success. The lack of long-term planning is another concern. The aftermath of the Iraq war, the lack of controls to avoid the financial crisis of 2008, the funding and management of the NHS, Brexit negotiations – it goes on and on.

It is sad that politicians are viewed in this way, because many are hard-working, public spirited people who enter politics to create a better society, both on a local and national level, through their constituency work and at Parliament.

On the one hand, you need collective responsibility, but too often, politicians are forced to support their party and make statements that are not in line with their personal views and the public can often see through an approach to which they are not committed. Also, it is a turn-off when they refuse to answer a question that is within their remit. Honesty also comes into question when the public are not confronted with the true position because the problem is worse than originally feared.

The general public do not feel that they are being heard and that their problems mean much or have any chance of being addressed. As President Bill Clinton commented, *"The world is in a period of extreme resentment."* Unfortunately, these concerns seem to have resulted in the emergence of far-right movements in Europe and far-left racism.

As Yale political scientist Professor Jacob Hacker commented, *"Many progressives believe in a role for government that is pretty fundamental. But they have lost faith in their capacity to achieve it... The era of big government is over. But we cannot go back to the time when our citizens were left to fend for themselves."*

Sanford Weill (previous chairman and CEO of Citigroup) commented that, in his view, real people had to step in and solve public problems, because the government was too broke and incapable and not up to the task.

When he started in public office, President Clinton believed public problems were best solved through public service and collective action. During his White House years, though, and even more decisively afterward, he had been won over by the theory that it was preferable to solve problems through markets and partnerships among entities, private and public, which would find areas of common ground and work together on win-win solutions.

State finances

So who has the funds and the will to provide the finance? The UK general government gross debt was £1,763 billion at 31st March

2018, equivalent to 85.6% of gross domestic product; 25.6% above the reference value of 60% set out in the Protocol on the Excessive Deficit Procedure. The debt increased further to £1,821 billion by 31st March 2019.[78]

The Brexit debate has not helped the government to focus on some of the key issues facing UK society, such as how we finance and run the NHS, social care, knife crime, funding the police, house building, providing for the state pension in an ageing population, improving the infrastructure, climate change and many other issues.

There was a general consensus that, based on an authoritative report produced by the think tank The Institute for Public Policy Research, the NHS needs an estimated £50 billion extra by 2030, together with £25 billion in productivity savings.[79]

Between 2010 and 2018, council spending was cut by a fifth. Local councils have been squeezed harder than many of the other big public services such as health, schools and defence. Local councils are responsible for funding and delivering social care for adults and children at a time when the cost of social care is increasing as the population ages. It is therefore unsurprising that 80% of councils were not confident in the sustainability of local government finance.[80]

Projected revenue and expenditure

The UK government's 2018 budgeted revenue and expenditure provides a guide as to where the money goes and whether there is

[78] The Office for National Statistics.
[79] Report 'The NHS needs more money – but how much?', health editor Hugh Pym, BBC News, 26th April 2018.
[80] Article 'The present model of funding for local government is unsustainable', Paul Johnson, director of the Institute for Fiscal Studies, *The Times*, 18th February 2019.

scope to obtain funds. The revenue was projected to be £769 billion and expenditure £809 billion, so that the deficit of £40 billion would add to the country's debt.

The main areas of revenue were:

- Income tax and National Insurance £319bn (41%);
- VAT £145bn (19%);
- Other taxes and corporation tax £141bn (18%);
- The balance, including excise duties, council tax and business rates £164bn (22%).

The main areas of expenditure were:

- Social protection £253bn (31%);
- Health £155bn (19%);
- Education £102bn (13%);
- The balance £299bn (37%).

The balance of expenditure included defence, debt interest (at £41bn a year), transport, public social services (£32bn), housing and environment (£31bn), industry, agriculture and employment.

It has been argued that one weakness of our system of public accounts is that they disclose the value of debt incurred but not the value of assets created. The argument continues that we should create a national infrastructure fund that values additional expenditure on infrastructure such as housing and transport, as well as the additional debt acquired. However, you still come back to the question: how do you finance the debt repayments and interest? You still need to compare your income to your expenditure, otherwise debt levels continue to rise.

To put it another way, let's assume that you own a house worth £500,000 with a £300,000 mortgage paying 6% a year to cover interest and loan repayments and receive £50,000 a year from earnings and savings that just about cover your total annual expenses, including the mortgage. You may be tempted to trade up and buy a more expensive house for say £1 million, but that would increase the debt by £500,000, resulting in additional interest of £30,000 and higher capital repayments. Where would that money come from?

In an ideal world, the state would find the money needed to cut youth homelessness, but as you can see, it is already running a deficit, with more money needed for other sectors. In the short-term, it can increase debt to provide greater funds for the NHS, long-term care, housing, education, the homeless provision, among other needs, but ultimately you cannot go on living beyond your means. Of course, you can increase your income as an individual by getting a better paid job, just as the state can increase its top line by helping to create more economic growth in the economy, leading to more money becoming available and higher collections in tax, but it is rash to plan for greater income before it is likely to arise.

I would be happy to be convinced that the state is likely to provide all the necessary funding to permanently reduce youth homeless-ness, but am currently of the view that this is unlikely, in the near future.

Taxation

We should remember that it is entrepreneurs, not politicians, who create wealth through developing businesses that employ millions of people in the UK. Through these businesses they generate corporate and employment taxes that fund the public services on which we all rely.

So what about raising taxes to fund the additional needs of the state? This has been debated on numerous occasions and the results can be counter-intuitive.

In December 1974, Professor Laffer had dinner at a Washington restaurant with three officials in President Gerald Ford's government – Dick Cheney (later vice president), Donald Rumsfeld (later defence secretary during the Iraq war) and Jude Wanniski. That month, Ford was proposing a 5% tax surcharge as part of a programme to bring inflation under control. It was widely assumed that a 5% tax increase would automatically lead to 5% more revenue. On a restaurant napkin, Laffer drew a diagram to explain why that was not necessarily so. Laffer traced the idea back to the Muslim philosopher Ibn Khaldun and, more recently, to John Maynard Keynes.

The basic argument was that if you set the tax rate at zero, you would obviously collect nothing. Likewise, if you set the tax rate at 100%, you would also collect nothing, as no one would have any incentive to work. Between zero and 100% there was a curve, because for quite a long time, revenues rose as taxes went up, but at some point, it started to decline, until you ended up with nothing again.

What Laffer emphatically did not say was that every tax cut generated more revenue. It just depended on where you were on the curve. Where any particular tax might be on the curve at any time is open to debate, but what you cannot debate is that there *is* a curve.

In recent times, in the UK, capital gains tax was at a modest 18%. Under pressure from the Liberal Democrats, George Osborne put it up to 28%, with the result that CGT fell from £4.3 billion in 2011-12 to £3.9 billion the following year and continued to fall, despite rising shares and property values.[81]

Currently, although the basic tax rate is relatively low, a high proportion is collected through the top rates of 40%, rising to 45% for earnings over £150,000. In addition, employees pay

---

[81] Article 'Want to raise more money, Chancellor? Then cut taxes', Matthew Lynn, *The Telegraph*, 22nd December 2014.

National Insurance of 2% on income above just over £50,000, while the employer pays 13.8%. What is difficult to assess is at what point a tax increase results in a sufficient disincentive to prevent more money being collected.

I recall a conversation with a client in the early 1980s when the top rate of tax fell from 83% to 60% (at that time, there was also an investment income surcharge, so the top rate of tax on unearned income had been 98%). The client felt that this was a tax burden he could accept. Later, tax reliefs were phased out and the top rate fell further, to 40%.

The problem is that higher rate taxpayers have become used to rates below 50% and a tax rise, where more than half of your earnings are taken by the government, could result in a sufficient disincentive to see the rise not achieve its aim of adding funds and could even reduce money to the Exchequer.

The issue of offshore tax havens is very unpopular among the general public, as there is a feeling that there is one rule for the poor and another for the rich, who can arrange their affairs to avoid paying their share. The world does not operate on a standard tax structure and it is difficult for any government to find ways to create legislation that overcomes the loss to the Exchequer through the use of tax havens. However, you can see, from the huge sums collected from taxes, that the government must take all possible steps to ensure that those who operate in the UK pay their fair share of taxes.

If the electorate were to be given a true assessment of the financial position of the country, politicians may be pleasantly surprised at the willingness to accept some financial pain if it is the right course of action and there was a belief that the money would be managed efficiently.

We need to appreciate the true level of money needed if we are to properly run the NHS and the structural changes that may be needed in the process. We need to accept that medical science has created a greater life expectancy, so the ongoing funding of the state pension requires further examination. We must adequately fund our education system. The police need more money to control our streets. The Crown Prosecution Service is badly underfunded. Controlling climate change will have a financial impact. Houses need to be built. We need a transport infrastructure to allow us to compete more effectively.

The homeless crisis needs a resolution, but where is it in the pecking order? Just getting people off the streets while ignoring them when they become part of the hidden homeless population is not the answer. It perpetuates the dishonest approach to a complex issue.

The financial crash of 2008 left the government of the day with a problem. If no cuts were made, the country's debt was likely to be unsustainable. This could lead to a collapse of the pound, with the current generation passing on too high a burden to the next. Debt repayments would be too painful and this would be worsened if interest rates rose from the then comparatively low level. On the other hand, the austerity cuts that were made have led to the under-funding of various social services.

We were between a rock and a hard place, but I do not believe that the public fully understood that problem, nor did they buy into the proposed best way forward. We are still suffering from the financial crash and need to rebuild our social services and the economy at a time when there is concern about low growth rates in the UK and across the globe.

We may be approaching a time when increased taxes at a level that will not prove to be counter-productive may be worth considering, but this may only be a part of the solution. A better partnership between the state and the private sector may also assist. Obviously, high economic growth will aid the healing process.

The position would be helped if we were led by a prime minister and government who had the trust of the people and could effectively communicate the action needed, with regular updates showing how we are performing against the various targets set. Creative accounting which shows, for example, waiting NHS times falling when the true picture is rather different, will only damage the process. This is easier to achieve with small projects than national initiatives.

Finally, on tax, there are notable initiatives to encourage charitable giving. Assets can be gifted to charity, free from capital gains and inheritance tax. Gift Aid allows the charity to reclaim the basic rate of tax and the donor the higher rate, so that a gift that generates say £100 to charity costs a 40% higher rate taxpayer only £60.

Money and politics

Politics clearly has an effect upon the money made available for social services. For many years, politics has been dominated by the two main parties, but with the public's disaffection with their recent performance over Brexit and concerns over the extremists from both the right and left, comes the emergence of a new centrist grouping of politicians seeking a new home.

The Conservatives have a reputation for being sound on the economy but less interested in the poor, while many feel that Labour cannot be trusted with the economy but do want to see a fairer society. The Conservatives will claim that austerity was caused by the economic mess left by Labour (remember the note from Labour's Liam Byrne, chief secretary to the Treasury under Gordon Brown to his successor, "I'm afraid there is no money"?) while Labour blame the current problems on the cut in services by the Tories.

The constant blame game solves nothing. The system seems designed to produce short-termism instead of long-term planning.

The political parties are, too often, afraid to level with the people and tell them the facts, in case they do not like the medicine that they may need to take to cure society's ills. Targets that have been set have been broken so often that you have to question whether they were realistic in the first place.

In the UK, we are facing a number of troubling issues and may need a wake-up call to deal with them effectively. Poverty, unemployment, a lack of opportunity, knife crime, gang membership, substance abuse, a changing workplace, a widening of the gulf between the 'haves' and 'have nots', climate change, funding and supporting an ageing population, the NHS, police protection... The list is long and the public are losing faith in politicians to respond to their needs.

The UK is positioned well as a service and financial centre, located within easy reach of Europe and between the US and Asia. However, it is sad that, over the decades, our manufacturing capacity has fallen on the world stage.

A table comparing the leading countries on manufacturing output in 2015 was produced and showed China in first place, with manufacturing output at $2,010 billion (27% of its national output). The US was in second place: $1,867 billion (12%), Japan third: $1,063 billion (19%) and Germany fourth: $700 billion (23%). There is quite a gap before you come to the UK. France and Italy are ahead and the UK comes ninth, with $244 billion; just 10% of overall national output and just 2% of the global manufacturing output. In terms of employment, just over three million people were employed in the UK manufacturing sector (9.5% of the workforce) as compared to 7.9 million in Germany (19% of the workforce).[82]

---

[82] Report 'Global manufacturing scorecard: How the US compares to 18 other nations', Darrell M West and Christian Lansang, Brookings, 10th July 2018, United Nations Conference on Trade and Development, 2015, International Labour Organisation, 2017.

Going forward, the position need not be bleak if we can recover our position on the world stage through creative engineering and technological initiatives. However, we need to level with people and have a realistic programme to deal with the challenges through a national approach as part of a global response to the issues of the day.

While there is only so much wastage in the cost line of the UK profit and loss account that can be cut, and a great demand to increase our annual costs, we need to increase the top line by driving up our outputs, which will enable us to provide the appropriate level of social services. This may seem obvious, but those in government have to recognise that encouraging wealth creation rather than taking short-term populist measures to hit the business community will only exacerbate our problems. Wealth distribution is more likely to come about if we treat the ultra-high net worth who give back to society with the respect that they deserve.

So what does this have to do with youth homelessness? Well, we know that the chancellor has to avoid running up excessive debts that can never be repaid and result in the UK losing credibility with the resulting rise in interest charges. It would obviously help if economic growth rises so as to increase 'the top line'.

The Treasury will receive demands from various departments for money to support the NHS, schools, the police, infrastructure etc. Therefore it is important that we identify how much more money is available to support HYP and the funds at local authority level that support the benefit system. Is there a case to be made to the public to increase taxes while not disincentivising wealth creation? Even if there is a desire to provide more funds from the state, how sustainable is the package if there is a change of government?

We are told that austerity is coming to an end but it is difficult to know just how much will be made available and the likely allocation between different departments. In the absence of a clear direction from the government and a consensus across the parties, we can only assume that we will continue to see UK governments continuing to fudge the issue, that we cannot expect enough funding from the state to seriously reduce homelessness and that the problem will not be solved by an increase in tax rates leading to additional funding.

Overseas approaches

So what can we learn from other countries when it comes to tackling homelessness? Finland is held up as a role model. Although its population of 5.5 million (2017) is less than one-tenth of the UK, it provides an approach that can be replicated in a larger country.

Finland has all but eradicated rough sleeping and housed a significant number of long-term homeless people. It has done this by giving homeless people permanent housing as soon as they become homeless, rather than muddling along with various services that may eventually result in an offer of accommodation. It was being considered by the then communities secretary Sajiv Javid.[83]

This Housing First approach of providing a stable home and individually tailored support was adopted in Finland with great results. Investments were made to provide affordable housing and shelters were converted into supported housing units. New services and methods of help were developed to match the multiple needs of individual tenants.

There was a strong political will to find new solutions and while there were a few local reactions concerning the location of new service facilities, they were mainly overcome by open interaction with the neighbourhoods. They found that stable living conditions

---

[83] Report 'What can the UK learn from how Finland solved homelessness?', Dawn Foster, *The Guardian*, 22nd March 2017.

enabled the use of mainstream services instead of using expensive emergency services and saved money in the long-term.

In Finland, the focus of the national strategy was clear from the start. The city-specific implementation plans included concrete objectives and resources to meet them. Also, in Finland, housing guidance has proved to be an effective way of preventing evictions. Financial advice, debt settlement and rapidly allocated assistance, supplemented with psychosocial case management were used nationally as well as in the private rental sector.[84]

The move towards Housing First has been slower in the UK than in some countries, including France, most of the Scandinavian countries, Canada, and the US. There are some risks that hyperbole will surround Housing First, presenting it as 'the solution' to homelessness rather than part of a wider, integrated and comprehensive strategic approach.

There is a need for a balanced debate, to consider what can be learned from Housing First in the UK, to think through how it is best employed in the UK and to look at those countries that are moving towards a functional zero in homelessness and the ways in which they have incorporated Housing First within integrated strategies that employ a mix of service models.[85]

---

[84] Publication 'The Finnish Homelessness Strategy, An International review', Pleace N, Culhane D, Granfelt R and Knutagard M, 2015.

[85] Publication 'Using Housing First in Integrated Homeless Strategies – a review of the evidence', Nigel Pleace, University of York, February 2018, Johnsen, S and Teixeira, L. (2012) Doing it already? stakeholder perceptions of Housing First in the UK. International Journal of Housing Policy, 12 (2) 183-203), DIHAL (2016) The experimental programme. 'Un chez-soi d'abord' Housing First main results – 2011/2015. Paris: DIHAL., Goering P, Veldhuizen S, Watson A, Adair C, Kopp B, Latimer E, Nelson G, MacNaughton E, Streiner D and Aubry T (2014) National at Home/Chez Soi Final Report, Calgary, AB: Mental Health Commission of Canada, Padgett D K, Henwood B F and Tsemberis S (2016) Housing First: Ending (Source: Article 'The Finnish Homeless Strategy for Housing Futures' as summarised by Josh Crites). The references in 86 to 89

Danish accommodation-based services will use trained social workers, a highly integrated package of inter-agency support and a very high staff-to-service-user ratio.[86] However, an Italian homelessness service is not currently considered to have anything like that level of resources.[87] The UK and Italy have something in common. Funding is comparatively scarce and unreliable.[88]

In Finland, all branches of government and the non-profit world work together in a unified manner with national goals. Within this strong partnership exist goals on how many units should be developed or acquired to combat homelessness. The coordination between all levels of government with a comprehensive strategy in Finland was the major difference between the programmes in the UK, US and Sweden.

In the US, local communities usually made the plans but there was no consistency across the country and these differed in complexity and content. In the UK, austerity measures affected many of the programmes as well as measures that gave more autonomy to local authorities. Many local authorities started spending different amounts on homeless programming because of the autonomy. This led to inconsistencies throughout the UK in various areas of the county.

The authors of the paper summarised the UK experience by looking at the issues of not pursuing a comprehensive homeless strategy and the lack of affordable housing units.[89]

---

below were also covered in the paper 'Using Housing First in Integrated Homeless Strategies – a review of the evidence'.
[86] Benjaminsen L (2013) op cit; Benjaminsen L and Andrade S B (2015) op cit.
[87] Paper 'Entanglements of faith: Discourses, practices of care and homeless people in an Italian City of Saints', Lancoine M, Urban Studies, 51 (14), 3062-3078), 2014.
[88] Bretherton L and Pleace N (2015) op cit.
[89] Article 'The Finnish Homeless Strategy for Housing Futures' summarised by Josh Crites, International Observation on Social Housing.

The goals in Denmark were as follows:

- No citizen should be forced to live on the streets;
- Young people should never live in hostels for the homeless;
- Periods of housing in 'care homes' or shelters should last no more than three to four months;
- If one is released from prison or discharged from courses of treatment, accommodation must be in place.[90]

Homelessness is rising in many countries around the world, so international cooperation and experiences of successful approaches need to be widely communicated. For example, in a 2017 article, Dave Hartley mentioned that his last two years spent studying in London, where the sight of rough sleepers is by no means uncommon, had not prepared him for the numbers of people who were sleeping rough in Madrid.[91] The Australian Homelessness Monitor 2016 also reported a rise in homelessness.

UK legislation

Bob Blackman MP is to be commended for first introducing the bill that has now become the Homeless Reduction Act 2017 ('HRA'). Its sixteen provisions came into force on 3rd April 2018, including:

- Extending the period an applicant is 'threatened with homelessness' from 28 to 56 days;
- Extending the existing duty on local housing authorities ('LHAs') in England to provide free information and advice;
- Requiring LHAs to carry out an assessment in all cases where an eligible applicant is, or is at risk of becoming, homeless;
- Requiring LHAs to take reasonable steps to help prevent an eligible person from becoming homeless, including helping to find a place to live;

---

[90]   Report 'The Danish Homeless Strategy' (115), Hansen.
[91]   Article for Life Sciences Abroad, Dave Hartley, 9th October 2017.

- Requiring LHAs to help secure accommodation, including the provision of a rent deposit or debt advice;
- Helping the homeless person to secure accommodation, including helping to resolve any problems encountered;

The provisions were reviewed by Centrepoint in its research report 'The Homelessness Reduction Act: Will it work for young people?'

The Homeless Reduction Act marks a turning point. It strengthens the duties owed to those presenting themselves to their LHA but also puts more pressure on these service providers. The results of a national survey of LHAs and interviews highlight a strong sense of optimism, with many LHAs energised to make fundamental changes to their operations, culture and approach.

While many are already developing innovative approaches, they feel restrained by factors beyond their control that will hamper the positive impact they hoped to make. This includes the level of new burdens funding, the housing market and welfare system. Almost all LHAs cited these restrictions as limiting the support they can give young people to access a tenancy. If not addressed, there is a concern that the positive impact of the HRA will not be fulfilled.

The extension of the period of 'at risk of homelessness' to 56 days will be a lifeline for many, but the timeline within which homelessness may occur will not be quite so clear for young people experiencing family breakdown. The complexity of the situation may mean that a family will require help with more than just housing, for longer than 56 days. For family mediation to be objective, the mediator must not have a vested interest in the outcome (i.e. returning the young person to the home, if this is an inappropriate solution).

The report identified various factors that are a barrier to reducing youth homelessness – for example, 86% of LHAs did not think that there is enough accommodation in their area for young people with high support needs, while 68% referred to a lack of supported accommodation .

The following response rates from the LHAs have identified steps that would help them to deliver their new duties of the HRA:

- increased burdens funding (79%);
- automatic payment of housing costs to landlords for anyone who has experienced homelessness (96%);
- an expansion of the exemptions from the shared accom- modation rate to include all homeless under 35s (88%);
- training for frontline staff (80%);
- good practice guidelines (87%);
- establishing a multi-agency working group (72%).

As mentioned in the Reform report, covered in more detail below, single people under 35 are often only entitled to a Local Housing Allowance at a Shared Accommodation Rate, which is the amount considered adequate to share a room at the lower level of the local private rented sector.

There was an overwhelming consensus among interviewees that low benefit rates for young people were not related to the cost of living and run counter to the government's commitment to prevent homelessness.

The Centrepoint report recommendations include the following:

- A shared accommodation rate exemption for all young people receiving prevention or relief support under the HRA to broaden access to the private rented sector;
- Extending the list of agencies that have a duty to refer, including the police and further educational institutions;
- Introducing automatic alternative payment arrangements for the above young people;

- LHAs to include a commitment to supporting young people in their council-wide homeless strategy;
- LHAs to consult with young people in the creation of age-appropriate advice and information;
- A review of council mediation services to examine their effectiveness;
- The government to provide tools and guidance to ensure uniform data collection across all councils so that data can be used effectively;
- The government to ensure appropriate future funding for the HRA when the current settlement ends in March 2020;
- The government to boost funding for private rented sector schemes.

The report concluded by stating that there was much to be positive about now that the HRA has come into force. Many local authorities are rising to the challenge and innovating in order to provide the best possible service to young people in their area.

However, it remains to be seen whether external factors, including the housing market and the welfare system, will prove to be an insurmountable challenge.[92]

Local authorities

The leading Westminster think tank, Reform, published its report 'Preventing youth homelessness – An assessment of local approaches' in May 2019. It provided a good insight into the position a year after the introduction of the HRA.

It reported that the local housing authority is often the last port of call for a young person in need. Young people often rely on informal networks of support, such as sofa surfing, and only seek external support at crisis point. One local authority stated that

---

[92] Report 'The Homeless Reduction Act: Will it work for young people?', Centrepoint.

young people only presented at the local authority once 'they have exhausted every friend.' According to the London Assembly Housing Committee, only one in five homeless 16-24-year-olds in London seek help from their local authority.

Poor awareness of their housing rights and expectations about the response they might receive from statutory services, as well as a reluctance to identify themselves as homeless due to stigma, have all been cited as possible reasons for young people not presenting to their local housing authority.

Several charity workers raised concerns that young people are still not being properly assessed, despite the introduction of the HRA. Multiple interviewees argued that although not always the case, within certain local authorities, there was an 'ingrained culture' that failed to take the concerns of young people seriously, which could lead to attempts to reconnect the young person with their family, even if it was unsafe to do so.

While the duty to refer in the HRA represents a welcome step towards adopting a joined-up approach to homelessness prevention, there is a risk that the duty does not go far enough to ensure meaningful collaboration between public services. In several interviews, local housing authorities with whom the statutory duty to prevent and relieve homelessness sits, said they still feel like they are 'carrying the can'. Interviewees have argued that this is because current obligations on other public bodies fall short of a 'duty to do something', and there is therefore the risk that the duty to refer could lead to a greater number of one-way referrals while maintaining an assumption that homelessness 'is someone else's problem'.

This lack of collaboration has been exemplified by the criticism that some public bodies are treating the duty to refer as a 'tick-box' exercise and passing young people over to local housing authorities. One charity worker even expressed concern that now the prevention role of some public authorities has been partly formalised through the duty to refer, they may have narrowed their approaches to homelessness prevention to only satisfy this legal minimum, whereas previously they may have taken a more proactive role.

Across the country, there is significant variation in the approach to, and quality of, youth homelessness services. The establishment of strong relationships with other public bodies and the strategies employed to prevent youth homelessness differ from authority to authority. Furthermore, the context in which local authorities are working, such as the numbers of young people at risk of homelessness, the housing stock available in the local area, and the funding provided through grants, varies across the country and can impact the ability of a local authority to focus on early intervention rather than crisis point prevention.

Digital services

Technical barriers were also cited as an obstacle to effective data sharing. Several interviewees argued that IT systems used by different local services are often not inter-operable, which means that it can be technically difficult to share relevant information. One local authority said that within their co-location hub, each service had a separate IT system, all of which were unable to exchange information securely and efficiently. As a result, it was easier for the frontline staff to pass over information in person, rather than through a specific IT system. For authorities without a co-location hub, however, this could prove to be a significant barrier to effective joint working. To improve interoperability and joint working, IT systems that are procured must adopt open standards that enable data to be accessed securely and efficiently across services.

Digital services, such as online one-to-one chats, crisis messenger services and group discussion boards can help to overcome physical barriers to young people accessing a range of services. In rural areas, for example, poor transport links and distances between services are a challenge to service provision and joint working. Furthermore, as homelessness in these areas may be a small-scale problem in comparison to more urban areas, it can prove more costly per service user to have a wrap-around service or to co-locate.

Through digital mediums, it can also be easier to reach young people at risk of homelessness. Young people are often reluctant to visit their local authority for statutory assistance and therefore using technology to access advice and support could appeal to them. A survey of more than 1,000 young people found that they are comfortable and regular users of technology, with 65% of the sample reporting that they use their phone if they need to know something urgently, therefore it is often one of the most effective methods for passing on advice and support.

The use of digital services, however, should not act as a replacement for face-to-face services or co-location hubs, but should be a further supplement to existing services. For certain young people, digital services will be unable to meet their needs and, as argued by the Carnegie Trust, digital exclusion is still a significant challenge for many young people, who would not have the basic digital skills to access services online.

To complement prevention work undertaken by local authorities, a national digital youth homelessness service offering advice and support could help to alleviate resource pressures facing local services and offer another avenue of provision for young people. This service would allow 24/7 access to support young people – a significant difference from the delivery of face-to-face services.

Personalised housing plans

Under the HRA, local housing authorities are required to produce a personalised housing plan for anyone imminently threatened with homelessness, based on a consideration of the circumstances leading an individual to become homeless and their ongoing support needs. In theory, this means that local authorities can offer clear and actionable advice based on the specific needs of an individual at risk of homelessness, such as how to access family mediation services or employment support. However, interviewees, including several local authorities, noted the 'huge variation' in the quality and detail of personalised housing plans produced so far, with not all plans being well thought through or realistic for the individual. In one extreme example, a plan was reported to have been written on the 'back of a napkin', with minimal detail. Although not the norm, this again highlights a significant variation in quality across local authorities.

Early intervention

School-based interventions, which typically aim to increase young people's awareness of the realities of homelessness, can act as a deterrent, by giving young people a realistic impression of what living independently is like on a limited budget. However, despite its use by local authorities and charities, provision is patchy, and approaches vary significantly.

The reasons for this are two-fold. First, the evidence base for this form of prevention is weak and more research is needed to understand whether fewer, more intensive interventions are more effective than universal, light-touch programmes; at what age young people should be targeted; and which methods of intervention are most effective. Reflecting the challenges of attributing long-term social outcomes to a specific policy intervention, to date, local authorities and charities have instead evaluated individual programmes using short-term qualitative indicators, such as improved understanding of homelessness.

Second, as noted in other studies and confirmed by interviews for the Reform report, getting access to schools to deliver such interventions can be a challenge. Because of the pressure on schools to deliver compulsory components of the curriculum, persuading them of the importance of this extra-curricular support and finding time in the school timetable to deliver a programme can be difficult. Where local housing authorities have been able to gain access, this has often been due to established, positive relationships between the local council and specific schools, rather than standard practice.

Accessing accommodation

High up-front costs for a private tenancy, rising rent costs and a shortage of affordable shared accommodation are all barriers for young people hoping to enter the private rented sector. Furthermore, private landlords are often reluctant to offer tenancies to people on benefits; in part because of mortgage and insurance conditions on their properties.

Social housing stock also represents a serious challenge to what local authorities can offer young people at risk of homelessness. Since 2012, there has been a decline in social rented stock held by both local authorities and housing associations, in addition to a decline in new social housing. There has been a 176% decrease in dwellings owned by local authorities in England between 1997 and 2018. There are also 1.2 million households currently on the waiting list for social housing.

The failure to build enough social housing, in addition to losses of current stock, has made it increasingly difficult for young people to access a social tenancy. Figures also show that there has been a significant decline in real-term investment and public grant funding for social housing, yet spending on housing benefit has risen from £9 billion, in 1991-1992, to £21 billion at the time of the report.

Funding and short-termism

As departmental funding, budgets and initiatives are relatively separate, it can be difficult to align policies across government to promote joint working. In addition to a shared vision of how to prevent youth homelessness that sets out the roles of relevant departments, there must be a synergy between policies and funding specifically focused on youth homelessness prevention. This could follow a similar framework to the Rough Sleeping Strategy, which has given different departments specific responsibilities and earmarked funding from each of them.

Youth homelessness prevention may also be hindered by 'political short-termism', where the most immediate, visible forms of homelessness are given the most attention. Crisis has argued that the public's understanding of homelessness prevention is poor, and that a 'crisis intervention' mode of thinking is dominant. This over-emphasis on immediate and visible forms of homelessness can 'impede thinking about systemic steps to prevent homelessness'. This is another illustration of short-termism that needs to be overcome.

Leadership

Strong local leadership has been key to determining whether local authorities have embraced the HRA. Indeed, examples of innovative approaches, early intervention, and joint working that were highlighted in the report were often driven by proactive individuals. The difficulty, therefore, is ensuring that a culture of prevention, which embraces early intervention and joint working, is embedded within services.

While steps can be taken at a local level to better prevent youth homelessness and raise the standard of support given to young people, local authorities can only affect change when it is within their power to do so. A lack of housing stock and current benefit policies, which adversely affect young people, have made home-lessness prevention more difficult.

Central government must support local authorities to prevent youth homelessness and must fund them to implement and sustain those strategies. To work in the spirit of the HRA and move towards a genuinely holistic and preventative approach to youth homelessness, joint thinking and planning across departments is needed.

The Reform report overview

The Reform report proposes 10 recommendations for the government to implement. It also found that although the HRA marks a step in the right direction, the extent to which it has been embraced as a wider opportunity to cooperate to prevent homelessness has been mixed. How local authorities have chosen to meet new duties varies significantly from authority to authority and, too often, good practice continues to be the result of diligent individuals going above and beyond their statutory duties.

For homelessness prevention to be genuinely seen as a responsibility that extends beyond the local housing authority, the legal framework needs to be revised to better reflect this.

As it stands, there is considerable variation in the approaches taken by local authorities to prevent youth homelessness, leading to a postcode lottery in the quality of service provision. This variation can be seen in the availability and quality of early intervention initiatives, such as family mediation and schools-based programmes, as well as the arrangements in place to facilitate collaboration between services.

A stronger national presence is needed to support local efforts to tackle youth homelessness and variations in service quality. Crucially, this national agenda must be cross-departmental, moving from the assumption that homelessness is a peripheral issue for departments beyond the Ministry of Housing, Communities and Local Government. Informed by an understanding of young people's needs, this national agenda should include the establishment of a national digital youth homelessness service. Efforts must also be made to tackle the structural causes of youth homelessness, including the lack of affordable housing and welfare restrictions facing young people, without which local efforts to tackle youth homelessness can only go so far.

For local authorities to implement policies to prevent youth homelessness, they must be financed in a way that allows for long-term planning and sustained transformation. Funding must be sufficient to support large-scale policy changes such as the HRA, and also to sustain non-statutory services.

Protected funding that is assured for longer periods of time can allow local authorities the security to develop effective policies to tackle youth homelessness. Central and local government must also be careful that the focus on ending rough sleeping does not divert attention away from preventing other, less visible forms of homelessness.[93]

State benefits

The various homeless charities have made representations to the government on improvements that they would like to see. The quantum of state benefits that may be available will be an important part of any funding plan and there needs to be a commitment from government that any such benefits will not be cut if we are to look towards permanent and sustainable solutions.

Funding the homeless

When seeking funding for the homeless and considering the role of the state in the process, we must look at the bigger picture. What are the current finances of the state? What is the current and likely future funding of the various social services? How will the UK economy be funded over the next decade, without excessively increasing its debt burden? Where does funding the homeless fit into the list of priorities? If the state is unlikely to be able to fund all the action needed to significantly reduce homeless numbers, is there a partnership between the public and private sectors that can be created to make serious progress? We will revert to these questions in subsequent chapters.

---

[93] Report 'Preventing youth homelessness – An assessment of local approaches', Reform, May 2019.

11

THE PRIVATE SECTOR

The range of private sector partners

As we saw in the previous chapter, the state has considerable debt and pressure on its funds and so I do not have confidence in any serious progress if we rely on the state alone; whichever party is in power. Also, with a potential change of government every five years and the occasional changes in the personnel at the head of a department, there is the danger of a short-term approach to produce results that make good headlines while not creating a sound long-term solution.

By comparison, wealthy benefactors can look long-term when considering a charitable cause; just as they may do when considering a business that they wish to see grow over decades rather than years.

It is my view that the lead must come from a joint approach between the private sector and the government. The private sector includes wealthy benefactors, charitable trusts and companies, as well as members of the public.

Charitable giving

Before looking at these potential sources of support, we should consider the costs to be covered in reducing youth homelessness and the amount raised by donations to charitable causes as well as the competing causes.

The following points from the Charities Aid Foundation UK Giving 2019 report are worth noting:

- The total amount given to charity by households reduced to £10.1bn in 2018 – driven by fewer people giving more;
- 64% of people participated in at least one charitable or social action, with 65% of people donating money;
- 48% of the UK population agreed that charities are trustworthy, down from 51% in 2016;
- If we take account of total private charitable giving, the funds raised increases to £19bn, allocated as 65.9% to individual and major giving, 13.2% to foundations, 11.4% to legacies, 3.7% to corporations, with a further 5.8% added by Gift Aid.

The following information is also relevant when considering charitable funding:

- The top 300 charities made grants of £3.3bn out of a total spending of £4.5bn in 2016/17;
- The top 300 grant making charities recorded net assets of £65bn in 2016/17;
- Total grant-making through different kinds of charitable foundations was estimated to be £6.5bn in 2016/17;
- This compares to government spending in the charitable sector of an annual estimated £15.3bn.[94]

The above information supports an approach of seeking to find major wealthy sponsors (ultra-high net worth individuals, foundations and corporations) as well as building financial support from the public.

---

[94] Report 'Foundations Giving Trends 2018', Cathy Pharoah, Catherine Walker and Emma Hutchins.

It is also interesting to note the growing charity fundraising through online and mobile donations that reached £2.4 billion based upon a report by Three as reported by Nicholas Tufnell.[95]

From the cradle to the grave

In 1992, I wrote the Stoy Hayward (now BDO) 'Guide to Personal Financial Planning'. It included a broad outline of seven stages of life, from a financial perspective. While no two people are the same, it can still be applied today. It is fully appreciated that the book was aimed at high net worth clients and many people are barely managing to keep their heads above water.

It showed stage 1: up to mid-teens, where a person is not normally working and has few responsibilities. Stage 2 is pre-family, possibly up to the mid-20s – working or studying but again, with few responsibilities. Stage 3: up to mid-30s – building a career or business and possibly a family. Stage 4: up to late 40s – a key time establishing a career or business with increasing expenditure on home and family. Stage 5: up to mid-50s – a high earning period, possibly with adult children and potentially reducing expenditure on the home as the mortgage reduces and children become more self-reliant. Stage 6: up to mid-60s (probably mid-70s these days), working towards retirement. Stage 7: from mid 60s (or mid 70s now) – retired.

The various stages give rise to different financial aims and implications. The overall approach was to earn enough to cover expenses in the mid-term and also save enough to fund retirement. The link to charitable giving is that it is often not considered until a person is confident that their financial position is sound enough for them to give money away. However, this can often be con-sidered earlier than is first thought, as the mid-term, when income is being maximised, is a time when thought could turn to 'giving

---

[95] Report 'Quarter of charity funds now raised through online and mobile', Nicholas Tufnell, Three, 27th November 2013.

back', as well as the later stages in life, when the position is even clearer.

The ultra-high net worth are normally very focused on building their business in the mid-term but can also be in a position to start helping with charitable causes. Some people review their finances at least once a year; particularly at the beginning of the year. If you are not 'just about managing' but earning at a reasonable level, you could consider how your finances would be affected if you built a regular monthly charitable donation into your budget. Charitable giving should become a subject that is considered at the earliest opportunity, if we want a fairer society.

Religion and charity

Religion has often helped guide its followers not just to 'give' but to be generous. Zakat, in the Muslim religion, commands a donation of 2.5% of wealth, while the Christian tithe is 10% of income, which is the same amount as in Jewish tradition.[96] It is very much a case of giving according to your ability to do so.

However, how many of those of us who can afford to give find reasons not to do so? Too often, we see success as how well we have done in business or amassing wealth, but in the final analysis, people are generally remembered by the ways in which they helped other people to have a more fulfilling life; whether this is our family, friends, or those who are reached without knowing their identity.

Competing causes

While children and young people were the third most popular funding charitable cause, behind medical research and animal welfare, youth homelessness is only a part of this category, and a

---

[96] Article 'Giving to charity – how much is generous?', Jake Hayman, *Forbes* magazine, 24th July 2016.

large proportion of money goes to the various children's charities. Also, in terms of the quantum of money, religious organisations receive a very large share.

It is accepted that money goes further when donating to charitable causes abroad, as costs in the UK are high compared to, say, building a refuge in India. However, it is also said that charity begins at home – in this context, the UK, rather than our family home.

With a society as divided and angry as we are now, it is important that we make significant progress to reduce inequality and levels of homelessness. Based upon the general response from the public over the past year, it is clear that they regard the current levels of homelessness to be unacceptable. However, the position is even worse than is envisaged, as the public generally do not see the 'hidden homeless'; rather the much smaller rough sleeping population.

It would appear that, with the increase in media attention devoted to the homeless crisis, it should be possible to promote the need for urgent action and find instigators for change.

Wealthy benefactors

If major donors are to be found at a level that will make significant inroads into the problem and provide the level of funding required, they will need to identify the importance of this work and the great outcomes that can be achieved with the right planning and resourcing. These successful funders would presumably wish to take an active interest in where their money is being spent, verify that the outcomes are appropriate and bring their expertise and drive to the process.

The use of technology has played a part in helping to create wealth for Bill Gates, and he and his wife Melinda have used technology to advance other charitable causes such as the development of sanitation and clean water toilets to reduce the number of children dying from dirty water in the third world. We need to consider how to use technology better to advance the work of reducing youth homelessness, such as in developing systems to better track those in crisis and how to improve some of the deficiencies in the benefit and further education systems.

UNICEF reported that malaria kills one child every 30 seconds; about 3,000 children every day. Over one million people die from malaria each year, mostly children under five years of age, with 90% of malaria cases occurring in Sub-Saharan Africa. An estimated three to 600 million people suffer from malaria each year. It is not difficult to see why Bill Gates wanted to take a major part in combating this disease.

In a 2015 speech, Bill Gates said, " *When Melinda and I made our first trip to Africa in 1993, it was really our first encounter with deep poverty and it had a profound impact on us. What we learned is that the private sector does a fantastic job developing advances in medicines, science, and technology that people in wealthy countries can pay for. But it under-invests in innovation for poor countries because the likelihood of making a decent return is so low.*

Most governments are risk averse too, and in poor countries they don't have enough money to invest in research and development, or even to get existing drugs and vaccines for people. So we worked with other donors, developing countries, and vaccine manufacturers on a plan to ensure that children in poor countries get the same vaccines as children in rich countries... So a portion of our work at the foundation is focused on how to address the barriers to engaging in effective philanthropy – everything from policy and infrastructure to helping other donors find ways to achieve their desired impact.

One example of that effort is the Giving Pledge, which Melinda, Warren (Buffett), and I got started about five years ago. We wanted to see what might help inspire and support others who had been very fortunate and wanted to become more effective philanthropists."[97]

14 people on *The Sunday Times* Rich List have signed the Giving Pledge to donate at least half their wealth to charity.

A good approach for the future is for ultra-high net worth benefactors to collaborate in tackling a social problem. Warren Buffett and Bill Gates were both on the list of the 10 wealthiest men in the world. Although they ran companies in very different industries, over time, they became friends and bridge partners. Warren Buffett was so impressed with Bill Gates' charitable infrastructure that he did not try to emulate it but donated his money to his friend's foundation. He takes an active interest in the foundation's projects but all the money is donated through the one charity.

Charitable giving

The debate about charitable giving has intensified of late. Sir Nicholas Serota, the head of Arts Council England said that 'social pressure' should be brought to bear on those who hoarded their fortunes, adding that, in comparison with Americans, British people are too willing to 'turn a blind eye' to those who did not give back to their communities. He added, "... *In America if you make money and you live in a community and you do not give something back, then the invitations will stop coming pretty quickly.*"

Sir Lloyd Dorfman, the Founder of Travelex, who has donated millions to cultural organisations, said, "*I would not go as far as to say that 'cold shouldering' should be a policy. I would rather*

---

[97] Speech 'The Power of Giving: Philanthropy's Impact on American Life', Bill Gates, National Museum of American History, Washington, DC, 1st December 2015.

that we should make more effort in incentivising and celebrating those who give. So it is more carrot than stick."

He cited a statistic from the Beacon Collaboration group to encourage philanthropy that out of 18,000 'ultra-high net worth' people in Britain with assets of more than £10 million, only 10% gave money to charity.

Paul Ramsbottom, chief executive of the Wolfson Foundation (which has awarded grants of almost £1 billion in the fields of science and medicine, arts and humanities since the 1950s) said, *"There does seem to be a debate about where we are going in philanthropy because levels of giving in UK society have remained stubbornly the same for a generation despite the state shrinking and despite lots of initiatives and despite lots of agonising and endless reports."*[98]

The excuses, according to many charity fundraisers, include that they are waiting until they have amassed their fortune before deciding how to spend it and concerns about the current political situation in the UK and that charities are badly run and their money could be squandered.

However, those families that have given large sums to charity have often endured and left a legacy for generations to come. The richest families that have survived the longest are often those that learned to give rather than spend, turning their children into responsible citizens rather than hedonists and taking to heart Andrew Carnegie's manifesto for the modern plutocrat to be a 'trustee for the poor'.[99]

---

[98] Article 'Shame the rich into giving, says arts chief', David Anderson, arts correspondent for *The Times*, 5th February 2019.
[99] Article 'When the rich stop giving they start to rot', Alice Thompson, *The Times*, 6th February 2019.

The level of charitable donations was identified by *The Times* article 'Richest Britons are failing to do their bit for charity' in October 2019. It reported that the richest Britons are giving less to charity than five years ago. An analysis of charitable donations from self-assessment tax forms shows that nearly two-thirds of people earning more than £250,000 gave nothing to good causes in 2018.

In total, almost one million people earning more than £100,000 made no donations, so that the over £250,000 income group averaged income of £454,000, with an average donation of £1,000, representing 0.22% of income. The most common donation by low earners was £270 a year; five times higher as a proportion of income. Donations by the rich have fallen by 12% over the past five years. The figures are distorted by a small number of wealthy people donating large amounts.

Matthew Bowcock of Beacon Collaborative, a charity that is working to encourage philanthropy in the UK, reported that the wealthiest are not doing enough and identified four reasons for this:

- *"Firstly, today's rich are mostly baby boomers who grew up in a welfare state. Many believe they've paid high taxes so the government should look after the poor;*
- *Secondly, Britain doesn't have a developed infrastructure to encourage donations. In the US, if someone sells their business, their financial adviser will always ask 'What do you want to do about philanthropy?' In the UK, only one in 10 advisers do that;*
- *Thirdly, charities are poor at building relationships with the rich. Donors often complain that they were not asked a second time and not thanked;*
- *The final issue is the lack of peer pressure. There's not enough other rich people doing it, which becomes*

self-fulfilling. The rich have forgotten the idea that if you make a lot of money, you have an obligation to society."[100]

This shows the challenge ahead but also the potential for change, if action can be taken to overcome the points raised.

Anand Giridharadas examined the approach taken by the ultra-high net worth in his recent book, 'Winner takes all'. He is concerned that this group will often *"favour the use of the private sector and its charitable spoils, the market way of looking at things, and the bypassing of government.*

They reflect a highly influential view that the winners of an unjust status quo – and the tools and mentalities and values that helped them win – are the secret to redressing the injustices... They have tried to help by taking ownership of the problem...

They know the problem and they want to be part of the solution. Actually they want to lead the search for solutions. They believe that their solutions deserve to be at the forefront of social change... More often, though, these elites start initiatives of their own, taking on social change as though it were just another stock in their portfolio or corporation to restructure. Because they are in charge of these attempts at social change, the attempts naturally reflect their biases."[101]

I can see no problem for these people with the financial means to be part of a well-structured plan to change society for the better and help to provide a long-term solution to entrenched problems, so long as they work with the other essential partners (such as government, charities and local authorities) in a coordinated approach. If they are the leaders in a well-structured and effective

---

[100] Article 'Richest Britons are failing to do their bit for charity', Andrew Ellson, *The Times*, 26th October 2019.
[101] Extract from the book 'Winner Takes All – The Elite Charade of Changing the World', Anand Giridharadas.

means of reducing homelessness and helping people to recover their dignity and enjoy a meaningful life, that should be encouraged and celebrated.

Bringing entrepreneurship to charity

The term entrepreneur has a number of meanings in the 'Oxford Thesaurus', including enterpriser, speculator, tycoon, magnate, mogul, dealer, trader, promoter, impresario, wheeler-dealer, mover and shaker, go-getter and high-flyer. 'Webster's Handy Dictionary' describes it as one who undertakes a commercial enterprise with a chance of profit or loss.

To become a mogul, tycoon or magnate, I suggest that the entrepreneur must also be a sound businessperson. Yes, that person needs to be energetic, and while there is often an element of risk taking, decisions are normally made after careful consideration of these and having taken steps to minimise the chances of failure. Certainly the risk/reward ratio will need to be appropriate to encourage a sound businessperson into action.

One of the benefits of having worked in a professional practice advising successful entrepreneurs is that you have the opportunity to study their approach to business and what makes them different from the average person.

They tend to quickly get to the root of a problem and find a way forward, whereas governments and other public organisations can become bogged down by political pressures, short-termism and a lack of a considered strategy.

What I have also observed is that the successful entrepreneur can normally see an opportunity in the marketplace, often after a study of the opposition and what needs to be done differently to attract new business. On the other hand, they can also see pitfalls that are not apparent to most people. I remember a number of different conversations with one very successful client discussing various business opportunities. That person took very little time to decide on the merits or otherwise. On some occasions, the entrepreneur would reject an idea without really identifying why – perhaps the brain had identified a problem but could not explain it at the time.

Some of the most successful businessmen I have encountered have not come from an Oxbridge university but are very much brighter in business than academics who may have a higher IQ.

Most are very focused and determined. When I questioned what they felt was the key to success, the answers were different. One felt that it was persistence while for another, it was attention to detail. There are generally a number of important criteria that entrepreneurs use to move from a standing start to a position of huge wealth.

So what does this have to do with charity or youth homelessness? Well, ultimately, I see a charitable project as a form of business proposition. You have to identify the outcome that you are seeking and work backwards to consider how this can be achieved and the problems that are likely to be encountered along the way. You need to consider the market and what impact you can achieve. How will the project be resourced? Where will the money come from? There are numerous questions that need to be considered before launching in and spending hard earned cash.

The larger charities may have trustees with experience of the issues that their sector will face, as well as professionals who can look at certain aspects, but not necessarily people with extensive business experience. The smaller charities may have less experience at board or trustee level. This can lead to well-intentioned initiatives not maximising their potential or, worse, squandering funds either through poor judgement or fraud. A business approach alone will not necessarily take account of social issues, but charities normally benefit when sound business expertise is at hand.

The public have heard enough cases of financial failure in the charity sector. In particular, it is important to look at the position from the view of a potential donor. A person with ultra-high net worth may have spent years of hard labour building a business. The route to success may have been painstaking, with them possibly having made mistakes along the way but also having reached a position whereby the risk taker of youth may now be a cautious older member of society.

Is that person going to hand over large sums of money to an organisation where there is no control over how that money is used? While some may be happy to do so, if they are confident about the way in which the charity is run, I would expect many other potential benefactors to insist on an active involvement in any charitable project. That involvement can be very positive, if it brings another level of expertise to a project, so long as the roles are clearly defined and there is not an excessive overlap. A good team should include people with different skills working together, but it normally needs a leader to bring the vision into effect.

I would expect any such person to want to see positive outcomes from their charitable work that convinces them to continue to invest time, effort and money in a project for the long-term. There is often a knock-on effect in that once one well-respected member of society has carried out due diligence on a project and can verify its positive outcomes, others will follow.

In my view, the key to seriously reducing youth homelessness (and all forms of homelessness, for that matter) is to engage some ultra-high net worth donors to take ownership of the issue while working with the government, homeless charities and local authorities so that their business acumen can be used in a way that will produce the best solution for tackling this problem and keeping homelessness at a sustainably low level. This could be by advising government, but perhaps the most progress will be made by leading charitable projects to reduce youth homelessness.

Charitable trusts

Some charitable trusts would have been set up by wealthy individuals who are still alive. However, there are many that have been taken on by trustees after the death of the founder. Some trusts have been in existence for many decades.

Of course, these trusts are bombarded by requests for money. Some will not entertain an approach, but seek to find their own way to make their annual donations. Others have a strict mandate and must adhere to their guidelines, which may cause difficulty in engaging in specific projects to reduce youth homelessness.

However, a brief analysis of UK charitable trusts that support children and young people indicate that they hold significant assets and award large grants, therefore provide a potential source of financial support. Within this sector are charities funded by the public, such as the People's Postcode Trust. In addition, The Big Lottery and Children in Need also raise significant money, although The Big Lottery may be more relevant in supporting youth homelessness initiatives.

Corporations

Companies can play an important role in funding initiatives and providing employment. The level of donations to charity from FTSE 100 companies has fallen by £655 million since its peak in 2013, according to a report published by the Charities Aid Foundation. Total donations in the financial year 2015/16 were £1.9 billion, out of pre-tax profits of £82 billion, CAF research found. The report stated that only 26 companies gave more than 1% of their pre-tax profits to charity, and that the top 10 most generous companies gave £1.3 billion – well over half the total.[102]

---

[102] Report 'Corporate Giving by the FTSE 100 – Bigger impact through better business, CAF, January 2018.

Public companies have a conflict, in that they are responsible to their shareholders, who are generally seeking to maximise profits and increase share values, and so allocating a proportion of profits to charity needs acceptance by the shareholders and other advisers in the city. Private companies, and especially family owned businesses, can be more flexible. I have seen the long-term benefits derived by a private company that allocated 5% of its profits to charities approved by the employees, where those employees became involved in the charitable projects.

The Information Hub published a list of homeless-friendly companies for those with criminal convictions. Some are well-known names, such as Alliance Boots, which has recruited people with convictions across all areas of their work. Compass Group are involved in food services, healthcare, education and sport and leisure. They offer opportunities for people with convictions and were part of a group of organisations who wrote to the *Financial Times*, setting out their positive experiences of recruiting individuals with convictions. Other well-known names include Marks and Spencer, Sainsbury's, Tesco and Timpson.

A quarter of employees at fast-food chain Social Bite have struggled with homelessness and have little or no work history. Co-founder John Littlejohn explained, *"The people we have working for us now don't want to refer anyone who would be a nightmare, so it's people they know are really ready to take a big step forward... You just have to use your instinct when you look in someone's eyes and see the hunger there to turn things around. There's a bit of patience required – there have been a couple of small anger-management problems. But by and large it's worked really well."*[103]

A study by Oxfam found that employers are more likely to hire an applicant with volunteering experiencing, because those jobseekers

---

[103] Article 'The homeless workers taking on Greggs, Eat and Pret a Manger', Adam Forrest, *The Guardian*, 25th March 2015.

are seen to be good team players and more self-motivated than other applicants. A number of companies encourage employees to become volunteers and provide working time to do so.

A partnership approach

I suspect that many potential ultra-high net worth people may have the will to help but have to consider how to do so in a way that is likely to achieve success while not creating a huge infrastructure in the process.

Assuming that such a person or family trust wants to take on the challenge of really making a difference, the plan would need to show how the targeted goals will be achieved and who will help and be involved in the process. There are numerous youth charities of different sizes and areas of specialisation. They may have the benefit of an existing infrastructure that is dedicated to helping HYP. However, they may be under strain to deliver their existing services while raising funds each year to keep them financially stable.

A partnership arrangement may allow the charity to work with the benefactor, who may be able to provide a vision, business acumen and financial support to the project. The other relevant parties can then be drawn in as required. This may include local authorities, property providers and suppliers of specialist services. In this way, the benefactor can set the tone of the project and keep involved as much as required, without creating an administrative burden or additional infrastructure.

12

THE PUBLIC

Initial contact

The first time that many members of the public are confronted by homelessness is when they see a rough sleeper on the streets. The initial reaction is often – how can this be? I want to do something, but what? For those who do want to help, there is a lot of advice on action that can be taken, including:

- *Acknowledge and engage* – Homelessness brings a sense of loneliness that erodes the core of a person's self-value, so a simple smile and a word of kindness can make a big difference to a day full of hardship. Above all, avoid stereotyping or stigmatising the homeless. There are many paths that lead to homelessness.
- *Alert the professionals* – Street Link is a government-funded service which allows people to alert local authorities in England and Wales to rough sleepers in need of support in their area. The service will contact professionals who will try to find them and help them to access things like shelter and food.
- *Give food* – When someone on the street asks for money, some give instinctively, while others struggle with what it might be spent on. For Rik James, who previously slept rough and runs Birmingham Homeless Outreach, money is not the answer.

"If they ask for money it's for one of two things – drugs or alcohol... Offer them food and if they don't take it they don't need it." It's his view that if a homeless person spends money on drugs, then the person who gave them the cash is party to the substance abuse. He adds, *"Just come out with food and hot drinks. Give them five minutes of your time, talk to them."*

- *Give items* – Former armed serviceman Ian Northcott founded 8% in 2010 to collect warm socks and chocolate for people on the streets of Birmingham. When he was a soldier, he often spent days in the field, tired, cold and wet. The Army insisted he put on a pair of clean, dry socks each day. Chocolate provides a boost, and other gift ideas which could make a difference include hand warmers, gloves, hats and books.
- *Man's best friend* – A four-legged friend can be some rough sleepers' only companion and buying dog food can help. The public could also put rough sleepers in touch with the charity's Hope Project, which provides free and subsidised veterinary treatment to dogs whose owners are homeless or in housing crisis.
- *The hidden homeless* – People could encourage those at risk of losing their homes to call the Shelter helpline, which is open 365 days a year, for advice and support. The government's Homeless Reduction Act 2017 places a duty on local authorities to help eligible people secure somewhere to live 56 days before they are threatened with homelessness.

Engagement

As we have seen, the perception of homelessness is often very different to reality. If you have the time to learn about the different paths that lead to homelessness, you can help.

Every person living on the streets has his or her own story. Some are highly educated and just down on their luck. Others are struggling with addiction. People have been known to have lost everything to medical bills, and some suffer mental illness – they all have value and deserve help.

If you are able, share what you learn with your friends, family and colleagues; possibly by blogging or writing about what you learned about homelessness. If you volunteer and tell others about your experience with enthusiasm, you can help eliminate misconceptions and stereotypes.

Supporting homeless charities

Ultimately, it is the long-term approach that will make the most difference. The easiest way to help is to donate money to a homeless charity. This ensures that social workers and professionals who best understand how to help the homeless will have the resources necessary to do their important work. Some people prefer to donate to an organisation that supports the homeless through their will, or donate to local churches, temples, mosques, and other religious institutions that offer help to the homeless.

Donating used or new items is another easy way to help. This could include winter weather clothing (such as hats, mittens, coats, and boots), new underwear and socks, travel-sized hygiene or first aid items and linens. Professional clothing and bus passes can help when applying for a job interview.

One of the constant struggles of homelessness is finding enough to eat – you could donate canned or boxed goods to your local soup kitchen or homeless shelter. Before making your donation, you may wish to contact the homeless organisation and find out which items they need most. You might want to provide toys for homeless families, as these children often have few possessions of any kind and may not have any toys at all. Adults could benefit from books, magazines, or other reading materials.

Supporting a project

We will shortly examine the main considerations and finance for a home with a view to supporting young people in crisis together with a full-time, live-in key worker and a full range of support services, with the expectation that current homeless residents will move on to a fully independent life over a two-year period. The ongoing funding requirement to support six young people through to independence can be approximately £40,000 a year. However, if the money were to be donated by higher rate taxpayers using Gift Aid, the net cost falls to £24,000 after tax relief, and so the annual net cost per HYP is £4,000.

One generous benefactor could cover these costs and take an active involvement in the project, receiving regular reports on the outcomes achieved. The benefactor may be happy to support the project long-term, as long as the outcomes are sufficiently positive, so that the funder feels that the money has been well spent.

A group of friends or business colleagues could fund a project of this kind, or a church community, or members of another religious group.

When considering the number of higher rate taxpayers, there were an estimated 364,000 people paying the 45p rate of tax on income over £150,000, up from 311,000 in 2013-14.[104] They represented 1.2% of income taxpayers in the UK.[105] The figures also show that the top 1% of taxpayers had a 12% share of total income and were liable for 27.7% of all income tax. It is estimated that 15,000 UK taxpayers have incomes above £1 million, of which 4,000 have incomes above £2 million. In total, there are now an estimated 30.3 million taxpayers in the UK; so a large pool of potential project sponsors.

---

[104] Report 'Highest rate taxpayers at record levels', BBC News, HM Revenue and Customs, 1st June 2017.
[105] As above.

Another way to fund a project is through crowdfunding, whereby a project or venture is funded by raising small amounts of money from a large number of people; typically via the internet.

Other ways to raise funds are sponsored bike rides, treks etc. However, the money will need to be available each year to ensure that the project is sustainable. These initiatives can be good to raise money for the start of the project, but this method of funding may need to be repeated each year to finance ongoing costs.

The generosity of the public can be seen by over £50 million raised for BBC Children in Need's 2018 Appeal. The money donated during the evening means that the charity has now raised over £1 billion since the first major appeal in 1980, all to help make a difference to the lives of disadvantaged children and young people around the UK.

Volunteering

There are numerous ways to volunteer your time. The sort of volunteer opportunities available will vary depending on the organisation contacted and its needs. From helping out in a winter night shelter, to volunteering at a foodbank or emergency drop-in centre, support is needed throughout the year.

If you are employed, sharing your skills with a job-seeking HYP is a great way to help them build confidence and access employment. There are many attributes needed by HYP when moving to independence, especially if they have not been in a position to gain certain life skills. Teaching finance, budgeting, cooking and other day to day life skills can prepare HYP for the world that awaits them. As previously mentioned, many retirees have a wealth of knowledge and experience that can be passed on at a time when the retiree may be looking for a part-time occupation.

Other ways include help with food distribution to homeless people, serving hot food at a soup kitchen, helping homeless people pay bills or teaching them a skill like gardening or playing an instrument. Many people have very valuable skills that can make a difference to the lives of homeless people.

Working in the sector

As there will need to be more people working in the sector, this can range from key workers living with HYP to support workers or specialist advisers. The level of expertise and relevant qualifications to be obtained vary with each position. There may be other roles that may require less study to join the team of people helping to make a difference.

Further education and employment

Many HYP have not had the opportunity to complete some aspects of their basic education and are in need of further education to be in a position to gain meaningful employment. Teachers looking for part-time work and retired lecturers could be of great assistance to people in crisis.

Gaining employment is often the final piece in the jigsaw. Most HYP do not want a handout but rather a chance to find a job that at least covers their day to day expenses. HYP with a criminal record are likely to find it harder to gain meaningful employment. If you are an employer, taking on HYP meets an urgent need. Many employers have attested to a high success rate when employing people who have suffered hardship and been given a chance.

Nightstop

Every year, individuals open their homes to young people who have nowhere to stay. This incredible army of people change lives by being Nightstop volunteers.

Nightstop provides emergency overnight accommodation for young homeless people who are facing a night on the streets or sleeping in an unsafe place. Communities and charities run the service in more than 30 locations around the UK, led and supported by the team at Depaul UK.

It is a unique project which relies on community hosting to provide a safe, welcoming place for young people in crisis. Volunteer hosts, who are ordinary members of the community, offer 16-25-year-olds a private spare room, hot meal, shower, laundry facilities and a listening ear.

In 2017, their 542 volunteer homes helped provide a safe place to spend the night for 1,403 young people. This service covers the critical time between a young person becoming homeless and the charity having a chance to arrange a more permanent home.

Volunteers apply to become a host and are visited and supported. Their training covers a variety of topics, including information about clients, dos and don'ts, practical tips, advice on maintaining boundaries and how to access support.

Volunteers sign up to a rota and choose which evenings they would like to host, on a completely flexible basis. All young people are assessed and checked before any placement is arranged. Staff are responsible for supporting young people with their long-term needs, including finding them permanent accommodation. Hosts are reimbursed for the expenses they incur and are provided with toiletries to offer to any Nightstop guests staying.

Accommodation

One of the key requirements is the provision of more homes for HYP. We have explored the possible role of private landlords who may be interested in entering into a rental agreement in a way that provides the current rental income, an absence of voids and has a social benefit.

If a property is currently empty, steps could be taken to arrange the tenancy. If there are existing tenants, it would be necessary to ensure that those tenants can find suitable alternative arrangements so that you are not merely bringing in one set of homeless people by making another group homeless.

There are many people who work with private landlords, from developers to estate agents to accountants and solicitors acting for property owning clients. Encouraging property owners to be a part of the plan to reduce youth homelessness is also a valuable contribution.

Signposting and prevention

There is a great need to identify young people in crisis and pass the details to the homeless charities that can help. Individuals aware of family breakdowns, teachers spotting issues at school and young people aware of friends sofa surfing can all help to signpost and prevent the problem from worsening. There are many early stage signs that can lead to youth homelessness, such as the loss of a job, general poverty and other problems in the family unit.

Community initiatives

As part of a long-term approach, I believe that communities will need to take a more active involvement in working together to find practical solutions to reduce youth homelessness. Many charities are already doing so, such as the way that Onside Youth Zones are bringing various parties together.

It is easier to raise funds when approaching those with money to support a worthwhile initiative on their doorstep, as compared to one further afield. It is also easier to break down the problem when tackled as a smaller project. You can also see more readily what works and what needs to be changed in smaller projects. This experience can then be passed on to larger projects. As the demands of the state grow, local communities will have to find ways to make their area a more attractive place to live.

It is amazing what can be achieved when a community comes together to help those in need. The play 'Come From Away' told the story of a tiny community in Gander Newfoundland where 38 airliners carrying 6,579 passengers were forced to land after the terrorist attacks on 9/11 closed US airfields. This tiny community of around 10,000 people (whose hotel beds in the town numbered only 500) opened their schools and homes and went to extraordinary lengths to help the stranded passengers over the next five days until they were able to get airborne again. The play recalls the great kindness and energetic resourcefulness the community showed their unexpected guests.

Community groups can be formed in conjunction with local charities and authorities working together to reduce homelessness in an area. Religious groups (for example, churches in the region) could collectively embark upon a project; possibly by encouraging wealthy members to provide financial support. A multi-ethnic approach works well, bringing together different faiths and businesses in an area to support a common cause.

There is a concern that, over the years, local problems that were undertaken at community level have been pushed up to the government and that more should be done within a community to address issues that can be seen within it; even if they are broad, national problems.

In the past, football was not a well-paid employment, nor did it generate much profit for the clubs, but now it creates huge wealth. I understand that, each year, before the Liverpool v Everton local football derby, the fans of both teams commit to helping the poor. In 2018, a total of 2.2 tons of non-perishable foods and toiletries were collected by Fans Supporting Foodbanks volunteers and staff before kick-off, with all donations going to the North Liverpool Foodbank.

The items collected resulted in North Liverpool Foodbank having an extra 158 emergency three-day food parcels to give to families in need, providing more than 6,300 meals for 630 local people in crisis within the L4, L5 and L6 areas. North Liverpool Foodbank coordinator Victoria Ponsonby-Martin said: *"This is a huge amount, and proves what our city's football fans can achieve when they come together."*

Everton Free School in Liverpool is a great example of a football club developing its role in a community. The school is in one of the poorest parts of the country and teaches children who are at risk of exclusion. Everton In The Community (EITC) is a flourishing enterprise, employing 125 full-time staff, 70 casual staff and more than 145 volunteers, working on more than 40 projects in over 300 locations, tackling vital issues.

Sue Gregory, director of youth engagement and employability at EITC, commented *"We can go into schools because the kids trust us. Football is a religion here. We can do numeracy and literacy, build a relationship. Kids know our standards."*

Denise Barrett-Baxendale went from running EITC to running the football club and said *"All in football should be challenging to do even more. I look around the Premier League table and there are really good people working relentlessly in their community departments to tackle significant issues, whether gun and knife crime, education, health, dementia, homelessness.*

For me, we still have to do more. We have to target the deprivation. Look at our city, the demand is increasing and we need to respond to that. It's not about the awards we win, it's about being pioneering, being courageous, doing what's right and proper in the community for those fans who support us."[106]

---

[106] Article 'We can tackle social issues: it's the power of the badge, Henry Winter for the game section of *The Times*, 4th March 2019.

The revival of community in a polarised world was considered in great detail by Raghuram Rajan in his excellent book 'The Third Pillar'. As the governor of the Reserve Bank of India and chief economist and director of research at the International Monetary Fund, he was well placed to examine the inter-relationship between the state, markets and the community in the modern world. He examines how to get the right balance between the three pillars that support society and views the state and the market as two sides of the triangle, with the community being the third side that needs strengthening. So, we should consider the role of the community in the UK in reducing youth homelessness.

Community can take many forms. We have been part of the European community but those in power did not ask us what we wanted. Most in the UK were happy to join up to a free trade zone. However, many did not want to lose the feeling that they were, foremost, members of the UK community and so, for them, the United States of Europe was a step too far. This can be broken down further into being English, Scottish, Welsh or Northern Irish, which becomes very apparent at international sporting fixtures.

Drilling down further, we pay our council tax to a local borough, but how close is that link? Within the borough, we may be part of a local association. We get very helpful advice from being part of a local association that updates its members on what is happening in the local area and where we may be able to find a good plumber or electrician. We may be a member of a religious group, so see ourselves as part of a community that transcends borders. Within the country, we may support our local football team or play for the tennis club.

As you can see, we may be a member of several communities at the same time. When seeking to launch a charitable project, it is easier to do so by engaging others who can help, and a starting point could be the local community.

The wider community is in a state of anger. While we are not engulfed in a world war, terrorist atrocities have been carried out between and against religious communities. The rise of populism is a reflection of people's anger, sense of being forgotten and concern about their own role in society. People cannot see a golden future for themselves or their children. Nowhere is this sense of hopelessness felt more deeply than if you have been abandoned and have no home.

Communities can come together, though, for the common good. By engaging communities, solutions can be found, if those who are able to contribute to the process do so. By creating more homes to move HYP towards independence, the community can come together. We can start with initiatives at a local level and engage the various communities within the area.

For example, many are aligned to their local religious group and may meet at the mosque, church, temple or synagogue. One of the side benefits of creating a project that crosses different members of society, be they Christian or Muslim, black or white, is that we understand each other better; especially when working together for a common cause. Ultimately the more time we spend alongside each other, the more we realise that there are far more similarities than differences.

If we produce a financial budget for creating a new home, we find that it could be achieved by bringing together representatives from different religious communities within a local area, each given the task of raising, say, £10,000 a year. Breaking the project down could make it easier to achieve. If well publicised, one project could lead to others.

Decentralised power can assist in creating local initiatives, and allowing local authorities the power to allocate local funds to cover benefit payments is a good start. It allows the community, rather than the nation, to become a possible vehicle for ethnic cohesion that can be replicated in other initiatives in the UK over time. When members of a community work together to overcome problems, they build stronger communities. It will also be necessary for the community leaders to overcome any resistance to change that may be found on the way towards completing a project.

These young people are homeless and therefore in a transient state. They may have come from a particular area of the county and have friends there, but have to register in an area to claim benefits. However, their ties to that district may be tenuous and, ultimately, while local initiatives may be part of the solution, the problem is a national one.

Political pressure

Another way for members of the public to become involved is as part of a pressure group to bring about change, and those with good contacts or a well-established media presence can all be part of the process.

PART IV

FROM HOMELESSNESS TO INDEPENDENCE

"You must be the change that you wish to see in the world."

Source: Mohandas Karamchand Gandhi.

13

PLANNING A HOME

Background

I thought that it may be helpful to provide you with a personal insight into some of the challenges you may face when planning a home, with a view to supporting a small number of HYP. There are many different approaches to achieve this aim and so this is an illustration of just one.

By way of an introduction, social workers will tell you that keeping children and young people mentally well includes:

- Being in good physical health, eating a balanced diet and getting regular exercise;
- Having time and the freedom to play, indoors and outdoors;
- Being part of a family that gets along well most of the time;
- Going to a school that looks after the wellbeing of its pupils;
- Taking part in local activities for young people.

Other important factors include:

- Feeling loved, trusted, understood, valued and safe;
- Being interested in life and having opportunities to enjoy themselves;
- Being hopeful and optimistic;
- Accepting who they are and recognising what they are good at;

- Having a sense of belonging in their family, school and community;
- Feeling that they have some control over their own life;
- Having the strength to cope when something is wrong – being resilient
- Having the ability to solve problems.[107]

The structure

It is important to set out the aims and conditions of the home. An important element to the likely success of the home is to find a charity that has a full service provision and the expertise required to support young people in crisis to achieve their individual goals of transitioning from homelessness to a fully independent life.

I favour moving away from the traditional hostel approach to create a caring home atmosphere. This needs the right support network, in line with pre-determined aims of creating a permanent and sustainable solution, albeit for a small number of people, in a way that can be replicated by the creation of other such homes.

While each HYP would now have a permanent home, they must work towards achieving their goal of moving to a fully independent life, and so it is expected that each resident will move on after an average of two years, to be replaced by another young person in need.

You should consider the age group of the residents and the level of their support needs. While some initiatives may favour a mix of ages and needs, I have favoured a focused approach, both in terms of age group and support needs.

The easiest place to start is with homeless people who have relatively low support needs. That is not to say that you should

---

[107] Mental Health Foundation website, 2nd January 2019.

not have a mix of residents but clearly the higher up the support scale, the greater the need for in-depth expertise on hand, and this may lead to a need for a smaller group in the home.

The ideal situation is to create an environment where the residents live harmoniously and even become a self-help group. Indeed, I have seen how this can be achieved, with some residents electing to live together once they are ready to move to an independent lifestyle.

The charity

The starting point for me is to seek out the right charity partner that has the range of support services needed for the young people. There are a number of homeless charities, but many tend to take on adults over the age of 25. If you are looking at a project for HYP in the 18-25 age group, the appropriate charities reduce in number. You then need to work with a youth homeless charity in your area or a national charity.

The selection of the charity could depend upon the role you wish to play in the project. In many cases, you may be willing to raise funds for a new youth homeless project but wish to play no further role once the money has been raised. However, if you wish to play a more prominent role in the project, and that is more likely to be the case with large donations from wealthy individuals or charitable trusts, you will need to be clear from the outset that the charity providing the support services is willing to accept your conditions. Smaller homeless charities may be willing to take a somewhat more flexible approach to obtain the necessary funding without compromising their requirements, but some of the larger national charities may be less accommodating.

It should also be borne in mind that most homeless charities, whether large or small, are under financial constraints, as many have had their funding cut. They will generally be reticent to take on a project that could lead to a significant financial risk. Also, they may want to be compensated for the time spent by their staff on the project. This is only reasonable, as charities must prioritise their own needs and be run on a financially sound basis. To do otherwise could result in a new project having a detrimental effect upon their core services to the homeless.

If the charity is to recruit a key worker, they should have a robust recruitment policy, as this is likely to be an important element in the project. Therefore, you need to find a homeless charity that has the expertise and broad range of support services and is willing to work with you in a way that meets all the needs of the relevant parties and is likely to last the test of time.

It is normally worthwhile spending time with the charity before committing to raise funds, so that you have a good working knowledge of the depth of their services. There are a number of questions that you may wish to ask, including:

- How many support workers do they have?
- Who are their trustees?
- How long have they been in existence?
- How strong are their finances?
- What support services do they cover?
- Do they have specialists that cover certain needs or do they outsource clients for say help with trauma or substance abuse?
- Do they outsource to local government services or do they use alternative sources?
- What are their safeguarding policies?
- What is their corporate and human resources structure?
- Do they work from a drop-in centre or meet clients outside the office?
- Do they have an outreach team that seeks to get HYP off the streets?
- If the home was ready today, could they broadly indicate the likely candidates?
- What role would they expect you to play before and after the launch of the home?

This is by no means an exhaustive list but it provides the kind of questions that I would want answered.

A key worker

Many homeless charities will have support workers who have a portfolio of clients they are helping. In some cases, the support worker will operate on an outreach basis, meeting the HYP at a café or some other public place. Other charities have drop-in centres where young HYP can access support. Some support workers are experienced, dedicated generalists covering the wide remit of support, helping the HYP to complete benefit forms, access a college course, begin the process of completing a CV or attend work interviews.

Some charities have developed their services so that they have not only a drop-in centre and support workers, but specialists in-house, who deal with particular aspects, such as educational support. In my view, this provides a more in-depth approach but requires greater funding. Many charities are providing relatively basic services due to a lack of funding while dedicated workers I have met would love to be able to provide a more in-depth service and, like many other services in this country, they are producing great work from a minimal budget and a low salary for themselves.

You can create a home that houses HYP together with floating support from a homeless charity. However, I have seen how much more can be achieved by having a key worker living with the young people. The problem is finding someone with the right level of empathy and expertise who is willing to live with homeless people. They can be found but need to be able to have a private life, as well. If you can create a self-contained flat within the property, this would help with the process. The key worker should also expect a level of respect from the residents, so that work hours are clearly identified and work outside of these hours is for emergencies only and should be relatively rare.

If the number of residents in the house is around five or six, this recruitment can be the most important aspect of the project; especially if a high-quality person can be found. The key worker needs a broad array of skills covering those normally required by HYP, such as support in helping each resident plan their path to independence and following it through. However, the key worker may also be able to help the HYP broaden their life skills and deal with day to day issues at the home; for example, liaising with the landlord. The key worker can also help to create a warm, caring atmosphere and assist the residents in dealing with any issues between those living in the home. I have also seen that landlords are generally happier knowing that there is a responsible person looking after the home.

Great care should be taken before recruiting a key worker, as it is better to wait and get the right person than rush to cover an urgent need. The recruit needs to earn the respect of the residents but also be disciplined enough so as to keep the right balance between mentor and housemate.

I have seen an overseas charity mould some residents into key workers of the future. This can be particularly powerful, when a young person in crisis can go on to earn employment helping others. Coming from the same background can also help in the process of winning trust.

Benefits

The ongoing funding of the project will often come from a combination of donations, grants and benefits from the state. While you may receive a firm commitment from a charitable trust or donor, you cannot fully rely on state benefits (as government policy can lead to a change in the level of benefits) and so contingency funds will be needed.

On the plus side, once a resident has proven that benefits are due, the income should be received, assuming that the current benefit structure remains in place. However, we have seen that the current benefit system is difficult to understand and the submission of a benefit claim does not currently result in you knowing how much is due until the payment is received. Even then, you may receive a follow-up letter stating that an overpayment has been made and will be clawed back, without fully understanding why. Also, there is no guarantee that the current level of benefits will be maintained by the state or that the benefit structure will not change again.

Despite these issues, it is important to establish the likely benefit structure from the outset, so meeting the right people at the local authority is a good start. Creating and maintaining a rapport with the benefit department can only help the process, if that is at all possible.

I have found that it is possible to find a sympathetic ear at the local authority and it is also possible to agree a level of benefits that covers three elements – a small income for the resident through Jobseeker's Allowance, a housing element and a payment for support. All this is to be wrapped up in Universal Credit, but if you can illustrate the level of ongoing annual costs, you may be able to agree a reasonable benefit approach. In addition the Homeless Reduction Act is on your side and should not be ignored when making your case.

When setting out a financial budget for the home, it is as well to consider the likely residents; whether they will be entitled to benefits and at what level. Any budget should be produced on a conservative basis and so I tend to assume that full benefits will not be received, for a variety of reasons, and there may be a delay in payment. For example, there may be difficulty in obtaining all the documents necessary to support a claim. The resident may start work and this may affect the benefit claim, but in that case, it is good practice for the resident to make up the difference through a payment for rent, if possible, as part of the transition to independence.

One approach is to calculate full benefits for the financial budget but then reduce the projected income to take account of some of the above reasons, so that you only bring in say 50% of likely benefits into the plan. If the benefit income exceeds the projections, then there will be an added cash buffer for the project, but what you cannot have is a shortage of cash funds that will make the home unsustainable.

Finance

If we assume that the income for the home will come from benefits, grants and donations from supporters of the project, you can start to project the likely income stream. To create a sustainable project, it will be helpful to obtain a grant that accrues over a three to four year period, and donors who are willing to commit for a similar period or provide a large donation in year one that you can effectively spread over a few years.

It is much easier to obtain additional finance once you can show donors the success of the work undertaken. Periodic reports that indicate progress made by the residents and a sound financial status will go a long way in convincing initial donors to continue with their support and obtaining new donors over time.

If the home is set up with a full-time, live-in key worker, you will need to build into the budget the gross salary, National Insurance, pension and cost of cover. You need to consider the likely weekly running costs such as food, additional support and sundry repairs not covered by the landlord. You may find that the home is to be less financially onerous than you first expected. For example, it is possible to create a home in London with annual running costs of around £50,000 (comprising £25,000 for the salary and ancillary costs of the key worker and cover and £25,000 for food and other running costs of the home). If you add rent at say £30,000, your overall cost budget may be £80,000.

The rent may be met by the housing benefit of Universal Credit and paid to the landlord, leaving £50,000 to cover. You may find that the resident mix is likely to attract benefit income to cover some of the support costs at say £25,000 a year, leaving the need for the balance of £25,000 a year to be found.

If you can also fundraise around £30,000 prior to the opening of the home and find charitable trusts and wealthy individuals willing to donate say £40,000 a year, your initial bank balance of £30,000 is likely to grow by £15,000 a year, and so not only cover contingencies but enable plans to be made, after a few years, for a second home. However, the key is to plan and fundraise early, and be conservative with any financial assumptions used.

There are various sources that estimate the costs of single homelessness over a year. One asked 86 people, who had been homeless for 90 days, about the services they had used. The report then used the available data to estimate the changes in service use that would occur if someone were not homeless and compared the costs that arose because they were.

While this was an exploratory study and not statistically representative, an effort was made to include single homeless people with a range of patterns of service use. Alongside people resident in homeless services for at least 90 days, the research team also interviewed those using day centres and other services, who had been homeless for at least 90 days.

People who had been resident in homeless services for 90 days, with their accommodation and support costs being met by the public expenditure for that period, tended to have higher costs. There were also some respondents whose use of homelessness services was very low.

The estimated costs of single homelessness over one year were £14,808 to cover homeless services, £11,991 for criminal justice, £4,298 for the NHS, £2,099 for mental health and £1,320 for drug and alcohol services. If all of these services had been used by one person, the total costs would have amounted to £34,516.[108]

In the illustration above of a home costing £80,000 a year to help six young people in crisis transition from homelessness to an independent life, this amounts to £13,333 per individual. If we compare the costs of £14,808 for a single young person accessing homeless services, this is slightly more per person than the home illustrated above. In addition, I would suggest that the quality of support is much higher with a full-time, live-in key worker, together with the support services of the charity.

On the basis that it is expected that each resident will have moved from homelessness to independence after two years, it appears to be a relatively low-cost approach, from a social perspective. The alternative is likely to be that these young people struggle to progress, costing the state significantly more, whereas they should now become valuable members of society, contributing to the country's finances if they were adequately supported.

Different financial models

Any financial model depends upon a number of factors, including whether the home is to be leased or bought, the cost of any in-house and external support, the estimated running costs, the agreed benefit structure and donations received.

The initial outlay will be a lot less if the property is leased, but it will result in an annual rising outgoing that will need to be financed. The location of the property will have a direct bearing on these costs, with London being more expensive than other parts of the UK and some parts of the capital being prohibitively expensive.

---

[108]   Research report, 'Better than cure? Testing the case for Enhancing Prevention of Single Homelessness in England', Nicholas Pleace and Dennis P. Culhane, Crisis, 2016.

To illustrate the different funding parameters, a property that can house say six HYP and a live-in key worker in London could cost £800,000 but half that in other parts of the UK. Indeed, with careful planning, a larger property with development potential could be found to house even more HYP outside the capital.

If we assume a rental yield of say 4% with a property in London valued at £800,000 and rental values rising at say 2.5% a year, the rental cost would start at £32,000 but reach almost £40,000 a decade later.

Alternatively, if a bank could be found to lend say 75% of the purchase price, donations of £200,000 would be needed to cover the equity. The model works best with a longer-term loan but if you wanted the £600,000 loan repaid after 15 years and the interest rate was charged at say 5% throughout the period, the interest and capital payments to the bank each year would be almost £58,000. However, at the end of the term, the charity would have an unencumbered property that cost £800,000 (and would be worth over £1.1 million, if the property value rises at say 2.5% a year).

The funding is easier outside of London. For example, there are parts of northern England with a high level of homelessness where a large property could be acquired for half the price of the London property, so that donations of £100,000 and a loan of £300,000 would be needed. The annual capital and interest payments would be just under £29,000, if the property were to be acquired rather than leased.

The benefit of the acquisition model is that it provides longer-term security and sustainability. The charity will not be subject to the possibility of the landlord taking it back. When the loan has been repaid, the housing benefit can help to fund other initiatives. However, there is a larger initial funding demand to find the equity for the property and meet the ongoing annual repayments.

The level of support required needs careful judgement, as greater support may be necessary if the needs are higher, or if it is felt that progress will be made at a faster rate. While this will add to the costs, it should be offset by the local authority agreeing an appropriate level of benefit support.

The property must be compliant as a house with multiple occupancy and from a health and safety perspective. This is likely to require changes that will need to be taken into account and various health and safety assessments, as well as regular fire prevention checks.

It is always best to ensure that the property is well-maintained and there will doubtless be repairs during the year, from a leaking shower to an electrical fault. These need urgent attention, so the budget should include a reasonable reserve for such costs.

The residents

The homeless charity should be able to indicate the residents for the house. Will you take anyone in the 18-25 age group or will you be more selective? Do you want to start with HYP with relatively low support needs or are you aiming higher up the needs spectrum? Will you concentrate on helping care leavers move to independence? Will the home be gender-specific or mixed? Some of these questions will lead you to consider the appropriate number of residents in the home that can be adequately supported and the likely ongoing costs.

Once you have decided on the likely resident mix, you may wish to consider how you can create a caring atmosphere in the home. This will mainly be down to the key worker and the residents themselves, but there are ways that you can seek to strike the right note from the outset. It may help for the homeless charity to carefully consider the available HYP who would most benefit from the home and for them to meet as a group before moving into the property. You are likely to achieve greater success if the residents are keen on the move and have indicated a willingness to use this as the opportunity that they have been seeking.

The property

It is helpful if the property can be of a high standard and well-maintained by the residents. This may be seen as part of a wish list, but if young people live in a dump, they will generally have no respect for their surroundings. However, if they are presented with a good property and understand their responsibilities, they are more likely to treat it as a home to be treasured.

The property should ideally be in a safe neighbourhood, near to transport links and other amenities. From the landlord's perspective, it must be well-maintained, and it would help if there was one person responsible for liaising with the landlord on any property maintenance issues. There will need to be clear terms as to where responsibility lies on any property repairs and all relevant parties will sign up to the terms of occupation and the rights of the landlord.

A licence for a House with Multiple Occupancy (renewable every five years) will be required and any work to obtain the licence will need to be funded. The landlord will also be responsible for ensuring that all compliance matters are met, such as HMO requirements as well as regular checks on gas, electricity, fire safety precaution etc.

If the project is for a home for six residents with a live-in key worker, the type of property will either need to be of sufficient size from the outset or able to be extended. For example, it could contain a small ground floor flat, six separate bedrooms, two or three bathrooms, an office, a communal kitchen and lounge. Residential properties of this size are not easy to find, but they do exist. Alternatively, converted commercial buildings, community centres or a couple of semi-detached properties may be suitable.

The residents would normally have their own, lockable bedroom and use of all the communal areas. If the key worker has separate living quarters within the house, that person can have the necessary privacy.

The legal structure

One of the challenges is to create a structure that all the relevant parties accept. If you wish to take a more active role than merely fundraising, it may be sensible to discuss this with the relevant party at the homeless charity so that you each feel comfortable and do not overstep the mark. This could then be written up into an agreement that each party signs.

One of the problems that is likely to be faced is the role of the landlord. If you do not have the funds to buy a property and are therefore renting, it is important that the landlord is comfortable with the process. The landlord will want to be sure that the property will be looked after and that a sufficient level of rent is received, with a minimum of voids.

Taking each of these issues, firstly, landlords are often wary of renting to people on benefits, even if the resident completes a form so that the income goes directly to the landlord. The property owner will need to be comfortable that the income will be sufficient and will generally not want to become involved in chasing benefit income. That person will also be worried that the property will not be properly maintained and so lead to costs and general aggravation putting the property back into its original state.

One way around the problem is for the landlord to let the property to a third party whose obligation is to properly maintain the asset and pay a set level of rent each month. This now puts the onus on the third party.

A housing association may be one solution but they may be difficult to find. The homeless charity or another donor charity could be another, but they would be taking on the financial and administration risks and many do not wish to do so.

In some cases, the worry about the risks may be much worse than the likely actual position, but it is difficult to convince a party to take on the risks before the house is up and running. There are no easy answers, but you should be able to estimate a worst-case scenario and work from that point in convincing a donor, or other party, to underwrite the risks to help to get the project off the ground.

You may have made conservative assumptions about the housing benefit income that may cover the rent. If you assume that benefits are cut in full, you can work out the deficit. If you have sufficient donations to cover the position for a couple of years, then this money could be used to meet any rental funding shortfall, and so the underwriter is effectively covered.

Moving on to the property; the landlord will normally be liable for major costs such as roof repairs. It should be possible to agree a level of maintenance that you would expect a landlord to cover and estimate the maximum likely excess if the property is badly maintained. These funds could also be built into a financial model. Therefore, it should be possible to get over these hurdles, with careful planning. It should, accordingly, be possible to cover the position for a couple of years, by which time the likely pattern of income and costs should be known.

To make it attractive for a landlord, there could be a fixed term of tenancy, say three or five years, so that the landlord is confident of no voids for a period of time and the third party is confident that the home is available for that period.

The lease could even be structured more like a company arrangement, with the internal repairs met by the third party and only external work on say the roof or outer buildings the remit of the landlord. From the landlord's viewpoint, if the rent is from a recognised housing association or charity and there are no voids (that occur as tenants move on before a replacement is found) this could be very attractive, while providing a benefit to society; especially if there is a commitment to the landlord to return the property in its current state at the end of the agreement.

The more you move any financial or commercial risks from the landlord to a third party, the more you have to consider how you can overcome its likely concerns. As mentioned above, this could come by way of the fundraising, by ensuring that there is enough in the form of ongoing committed annual donations by sponsors of the scheme.

Complete transparency as regards the finance is very important so that any donor can review the monthly cash flow position, if necessary. Also, a separate bank account for the project would help to ensure the integrity of the financial position and avoid any mixing of income and expenditure from this project with any other arrangements.

Conclusion

There are various homes that can be created, depending upon various factors such as the number of residents, the size of the property, their support needs and method of service provision.

A home could be operated without the key worker for the low support cases (and so the annual costs would be lower). You could have a one-bedroom flat (or just a bedroom and use of communal parts) for someone who works during the day but is on hand at night for any emergencies, in return for which the rent for the flat is either waived or reduced. Alternatively, the home could operate with floating support workers during the day only and a night-time emergency service available as and when required. You need to consider the position from every viewpoint – what is right for the residents, the charity, the funders and the landlord.

HYP come with a varying array of issues and while I am not advocating a strict list of criteria for each home, those with low support needs are generally the easiest to house, as a starting point. Those with serious substance abuse problems may be better suited to a home with specialist support services to help them overcome their addictions.

Clearly, the house rules will need to be specifically tailored to take account of the problems encountered by the HYP. If the home has HYP with high support needs, it may require a different support network and perhaps a more intensive approach, with fewer residents per key worker.

There could be a variety of other models for future homes. Over the years, there have been a large number of care homes built to meet the needs of an ageing society. These have been run for profit by corporations around the UK. What is now needed is the creation of care homes for the homeless. I am sure that many different models will emerge if we can engage the right people.

One of the problems with the small number of homes that are currently available for young people in crisis is that when you are alerted to a new case, it is likely that there will be no appropriate accommodation. Even so, urgent action is required at this time to move that person off the streets or from temporary accommodation into a more permanent residence, with support. As more homes are created, more rooms will become available, as residents make the move from homelessness to independence. This will result in much quicker action when young people reach crisis point, resulting in a better chance of creating a positive response and so avoiding a downward spiral that may lead to longer-term treatment.

14

ACHIEVING INDEPENDENCE

Moving on from homelessness

It is worth noting how lives can be turned around with resilience, support and persistence. Jose, 25, came to the charity No Limits because he was facing homelessness, dealing with depression, struggling with debt and had no family nearby to support him. He was turning to substances to make himself feel better. With their support, Jose made some big changes in his life and now feels hopeful about the future.

"My time on the streets was horrible. You are faced with trying to keep warm. Look for food. You meet people in the same boat, but they are not people you would like to hang around with. I met a lot of young people who were on the streets for all sorts of reasons. I lived in the woods for a bit and found myself lighting a fire under a bridge near a train line. I just broke down. Luckily a friend reached out to me who persuaded me to move near him, have a fresh start."

When Jose came to No Limits, he was referred to a housing provider and given the opportunity to use their laundry and shower facilities and get food while he was waiting for accommodation to become available. They also began to address his financial difficulties by setting up a budgeting form and prioritising his debts. *"No Limits helped me deal with the debt. I set a goal for myself – to get into university. I decided I had to stay focused on that. No Limits picked me up and gave me hope. They helped me find suitable accommodation and finally I had a roof over my head."*

Jose's true passion was music, but with his mood so low, he had no self-belief to pursue his dreams. As his confidence started to grow, Jose was able to secure DJ slots at some local clubs and pubs. He applied for a foundation course in Digital Music at Southampton Solent University and was successful. Jose says he is happier than ever. Now that he has stable housing and is starting to achieve his goals, he has been able to reduce his drug use and is feeling better mentally.

"I messed up before and I don't want that to happen again. I'm staying away from drugs and alcohol too. I have something to focus on and I want to set up my own record label in the future. I've got a lot of options compared to before. I still get low moments, but I manage to pull myself out of it now. My advice to other young homeless people would be to set a goal. Put 100% into it and there is a light at the end of the tunnel, but you can't just expect help from others. You have to do it for yourself".[109]

From homelessness to saving others

We often find that those who have been abused and neglected want to help others and move into the care sector. The case of Mariuma Ben Yosef is an inspiring example.

Mariuma was abandoned by her father at two years of age, sexually abused at five and again at 10. She was sleeping rough on the streets at 14 and eating from rubbish bins. She was raped at 17 but was determined to never let her victimisers win. She had an unplanned pregnancy at 20 and decided to keep the baby and defer going to acting school but instead she finished her studies.

---

[109] 'Joe's story; from homelessness to hope', No Limits

At 21, she was living with her partner and the baby and decided to devote her life to children who were, as she had been, on the streets. She had felt most alone on Friday nights and at holidays when families would normally be together and so she started making a Friday night dinner for some of those who used to sleep rough with her, and word of mouth spread. Soon children came from all over the country to have a hot meal and sleep in tents in her back garden.

One girl who had been travelling in India said that she felt 'Shanti', at peace, in the home. A guy picked up a pen and wrote 'Welcome to Shanti House' on the wall and this was the start of Mariuma's 32-year journey to build her charity for forgotten children and youth.

One night, a girl approached her and asked if she could talk about her rape and this led Mariuma to open up about her own experience. For the first time, Mariuma said that she felt a release of pain by being about to talk and share the terrible experience, and she wanted to feel that way every day. She did not fill the black hole with drugs or alcohol, but food, and it took some time for her to work through the past. She eventually started to eat better and look after herself.

Shanti House is multi-ethnic charity taking in Jews, Muslims, Christians and young people of any faith or sexual persuasion. 80% of the children at Shanti have been rejected by their parents – which Mariuma says is worse than being orphaned. The approach is one of mercy, not pity – in the Shanti homes, there are to be no drugs, no violence, no sex. The young people, aged 14-21, have to develop their plan for independence, with help from the Shanti team. They have to get up on time, breakfast and dine together and carry out their daily chores to keep the place clean.

Like the residents, Mariuma wants to continue learning, keep up the passion for her work and follow her dream. Over the past 32 years, over 40,000 children have 'chosen life' at Shanti House in its two properties with over 100 beds. Some children spend a short time getting help while others live there, sharing a bedroom until they are ready to move on to an independent life. Mariuma has been nominated as a CNN hero and Shanti House has won The President's Award for its wonderful work.

Sabrina Cohen-Hatton was nine and her brother seven when their father died after a brain tumour. This sent their mother into a spiral of despair and deteriorating mental health. Their parent's business folded and their mother struggled to look after them. They became destitute and the atmosphere was so volatile and unpredictable that, shortly before Sabrina's 16th birthday, she packed her schoolbooks, uniform and some clothes and left.

Sabrina slept in the doorway of a church in Newport, then tried staying at hostels, but found them to be neither safe nor welcoming. When the church was boarded up, she slept in subways and a derelict building in the city centre. One night, she woke up to find that a drunk had urinated on her sleeping bag. After a homeless man stubbed out his cigarette on her arm, she fled; leaving her schoolbooks behind – the most important things she owned.

Every day she went to school, getting the one square meal a day. As the scruffy kid with dirty clothes and holes in her shoes, she did not have many friends. However, she saw education as her way out; an opportunity to change her situation and make something of her life.

She recalled that when she felt powerless, finding any kind of control amid the chaos was incredibly meaningful. Still homeless when she sat her GCSEs, she somehow managed to achieve one A*, six As and three Bs.

Sabrina left school at 16 and lived hand to mouth selling *The Big Issue* and saving money wherever she could. She bought a van and slept in it for a while, feeling safer than on the streets, and faced the catch 22 situation of needing an address to get a job, but not being able to afford a home as she did not have a job.

After two years of scrimping and saving, she eventually raised enough money for a deposit on a tiny flat.

At 18, she had her sights set on a career in the fire service, driven by her ambition to help people during their most difficult times. Knowing what it is like to have the worst day you could possibly imagine, to be so vulnerable and lost that it feels like no one can pull you from the depths of desperation, Sabrina wanted to help, soothe and protect. She wanted to rescue people, because when she was growing up, there had been no one to rescue her.

She feels that the fire service saved her – it gave her a purpose; a career trajectory with clear opportunities for progression. Sabrina is now in her 30s, a deputy assistant commissioner in one of the largest fire brigades in the world, responsible for managing teams and developing strategies and policies to enhance the service, and married, with a daughter. You can read her story in her book 'The Heat of the Moment'.

From homelessness to head boy

While there is a debate in the UK about the positioning of private schools, one boarding school, charging £35,000 a year, has been accepting pupils from troubled families. Kingham Hill School is set in 100 acres of Cotswold countryside. It is funding a girl whose fostering arrangements fell through.

Julien Andre, 17, head boy at Kingham Hill, has been sponsored by Buttle UK since he was removed from a broken home at the age of 10. His mother, who had mental health and drink problems, was struggling to look after him. When he was younger, the pair lived on the streets in London for a year and the family went on to share a home with a drug dealer.

When Julien arrived at the school, he was five foot three inches tall but, due to his poor diet, weighed 15 stone. Now he is slim and fit, plays rugby for the school's first XV and has applied to Brasenose College Oxford to study philosophy and Spanish. As he reported, *"I was given a huge opportunity. I was terrified it would be taken away."*[110]

Resilience

'The Last Black Man in San Francisco' is a film with the lead part played by Jimmie Fails, now a 24-year-old, and based upon Jimmie's own story. The film shows Jimmie staring up at a magnificent 1880s townhouse in the Fillmore district of San Francisco, where properties can now fetch $4 million. For decades it belonged to Jimmie's family at a time when black people still lived in Fillmore, before the influx of tech millionaires to the district.

Jimmie spent his early years in the house with his extended family, but a combination of drug abuse and money squabbles meant that his family were unable to keep up with the mortgage payments and finally lost the property to foreclosure. He would spend the rest of his childhood bouncing between homeless shelters, housing projects and foster care.

In one scene, Jimmie finds himself sitting on a bus opposite his mother, who was a recovering drug addict, having been forced to give him up, after which they had only been in touch sporadically (he convinced his mother to play her part in the film). His father's drug addiction led to a chaotic lifestyle, with Jimmie staying with relatives when his father was in prison, or in foster homes, but often running away as he was unhappy in those environments.

With little money and taking menial work, adult Jimmie kept obsessing about his first house, returning to look at it, again and again. He would even sneak into the grounds and touch up the paintwork when the owners were away.

---

[110] Article 'He lived on the streets and with drug dealers. Now he's a top head boy', Nicholas Hellen, *The Sunday Times*, 20th October 2019.

Despite a chaotic childhood, he did well at school, as it was a place where he could succeed and have some stability. He would always turn up early for breakfast and took extra lunch so that he could eat later. He wanted a better life but had no control over what was happening to him. He wanted that control over his future.

In his early teens, Jimmie befriended Joe Talbot and moved in with Joe's family, who were fifth-generation San Franciscans. Joe's parents were writers who shared a deep love and nostalgia for San Francisco. Joe first suggested using Jimmie's obsession with the house as the subject for a film.

In 2015, they released a short promotional video and, in a month, raised $75,000 through crowdfunding. Jimmie had no formal training beyond high school drama classes. Industry interest picked up but the studios wanted an experienced actor to play the part. Jimmie and Joe persevered and, finally, they received a call from Danny Glover, a native San Franciscan and long-term political activist, who helped. Eventually, sufficient financial interest was secured and they started filming. This remarkable film won two prizes at the Sundance Film Festival and is even tipped by many critics for Academy Award success.

To Jimmie, the house represented a lost future; not just one of stability for himself, but for thousands of people in his home city whom, like him, had found themselves uprooted. He has stopped obsessing about the house, has just won his second acting role and is moving on with his life.[111]

George S Patton once said, *"The test of success is not what you do when you are on top. Success is how high you bounce when you hit bottom."* Of course, it normally takes a number of people and organisations working together to make one person's dream come true.

---

[111] Jimmie Fails interview on 'The Last Black Man in San Francisco', Ben Machell, *The Times Magazine*, 12th October 2019.

Chris Gardner was arrested for not paying $1,200 in parking tickets, imprisoned for 10 days and had nothing except the clothes on his back. He took on the responsibility for looking after his son and they ate in soup kitchens and slept at airports and washrooms. He eventually got a job and started his own brokerage firm that, in time, was valued at $60 million. His story was told in 'The Pursuit of Happyness', with Will Smith as the lead.

Tyler Perry was born into a dysfunctional family with an abusive father and sexually abused as a child. He took refuge in writing, and his play, 'I know I've Been Changed', was rejected six times. The costs left him living in his car but he persisted and the play finally ran in 1998. He is now one of the highest paid men in the entertainment business as a writer, director and actor.

Liz Murray was born in 1980 to drug addiction parents. Her mother died when she was five and she was forced to live with her father, who was HIV positive, and sister, sleeping on subway trains and park benches. Despite all this, she enrolled late in an academy, finished her schooling and won a scholarship, graduated from Harvard and returned to study for a doctorate in clinical psychology. She is a counsellor and motivational speaker and her 2010 memoir 'Breaking Night' was a *New York Times* bestseller.

A number of well-known celebrities have triumphed against adversity. For example, Oscar winner Halle Berry once stayed in a homeless shelter in her 20s, Ella Fitzgerald was homeless before becoming the 'Queen of jazz', while Hilary Swank lived in a car with her mother before winning two Oscars by age 30.

Other people have overcome poverty to become billionaires, such as Oprah Winfrey, Guy Laliberte (who founded Cirque de Soleil), Nohed Altrad (who came from a nomadic tribe in Syria to become French Entrepreneur of the Year), and George Soros who, after surviving Nazi-occupied Hungary as a youngster, has donated over $32 billion to his philanthropic agency.

15

THE BIG PICTURE

The global picture

You sometimes read headlines about how we can end homelessness for ever, but how realistic is this? We are human and, unfortunately, people do not always act in an appropriate way; whether it be to a partner, child, friend or fellow employee.

With family breakdown high up the list of reasons for youth homelessness, I suspect that the best that we can plan for is a major reduction in the numbers and a continued maintenance of that improved situation. If that is achieved, it would be a huge step forward.

To make significant progress, we need to plan well ahead. In business, I often worked on both a short-term plan and a long-term strategy. The short-term could be one year, to keep your eye on the immediate work, while the long-term could be rolling five years, or even longer-term action plans.

Whatever your views on the Chinese government and their human rights record, China has lifted over 68 million people out of poverty over the five years since President Xi Jinping took power.[112] A key to this success is China's long-term vision and planning.

---

[112] Article 'China lifts over 68 million people out of poverty in 5 years: Report', *The Economic Times*, 10th February 2018.

The best recent illustration is the 'Chinese Dream', setting the ambition and key milestones to the middle 21st century for national development. This long-term vision is backed by several sectorial development plans that are both pragmatic and feasible. Anchored in its tradition, China pays high attention to education and training.[113]

The recent demonstrations in Hong Kong and exposure on how China treats its minorities illustrates the frictions in that country. With a current population of over 1.4 billion, the world is watching to see how President Xi Jinping handles the issues that his country currently faces. It is always worrying when someone becomes president for life.

Africa has a population of 1.3 billion and most of this continent has been run by dictators who have stolen vast sums, leaving the people in poverty and their countries dangerous and corrupt. This, in turn, has led to huge numbers of refugees fleeing dangerous regimes to live in Europe; thereby putting added pressure on our continent.

There does not appear to be a force for good to bring delinquent dictators to account for their actions. The UN was set up with good intentions but has often failed to act effectively. The West has made matters worse, when intervening with military campaigns. The effect has been for some leaders to retrench, leaving a vacuum for extremists to fill. The homeless crisis could worsen from the current unacceptable position if the situation deteriorates outside of Europe and it could also be adversely affected if the European community comes under further strain internally.

---

[113] Article 'China, the power of long-term planning', Patrick Koller, 30th July 2018.

Keeping track

If we are to make progress, we need systems that enable us to identify and track the homeless population. This will require an understanding of the scale of the problem and whether various measures are achieving their aim. At present, we have a huge hidden homeless population; many of whom are outside the government's statistics.

Creating a meaningful database is not a simple matter, as it would need a link between the various parties, including the outreach teams, homeless charities, local authorities, landlords housing the homeless, benefit departments and government bodies.

As recommended in the Canadian research mentioned earlier, data collection on homeless youth will ensure that programmes and services are efficient in their operation and will help to measure outcomes. Its action plans included:

- Work with youth shelter providers to implement a Homeless Management Information System.
- Establish information sharing arrangements with youth-serving organisations to facilitate the single point of entry system.

In terms of obtaining accurate data or even an approximate number of young homeless people, I can only endorse the following recommendations in the report by Crisis:

- There is a lack of accurate and consistent data on all forms of homelessness across England, Scotland and Wales. The way data is used to drive commissioning decisions and service design also varies;
- We need a common framework to evidence and measure progress against the goal of ending homelessness for policy-makers, funders, and practitioners and help them improve

and standardise data on all types of homelessness across Great Britain.[114]

The HYP population

If we are to consider the resources needed to significantly reduce youth homelessness, we need a starting point. All the research I have read has indicated that we lack accurate information on the current youth homeless population. However, as mentioned earlier, I have worked on 200,000 HYP in the UK needing support. Over time, any plans can be updated to take account of a different sized population when more accurate data is available.

Potential costs and benefits

The Crisis 2018 report on total UK homelessness estimated that the discounted cost of the solutions recommended by Crisis between 2018 and 2041 is £19.3 billion at 2017 prices, with £9.94 billion needed between 2018 and 2027, at an average of £1.1 billion a year during this period. Interestingly, the report estimated that the recommended solutions will discover benefits of £53.9 billion, with £26.4 billion delivered between 2018 and 2027, at an average of £2.9 billion a year. Therefore, for every £100 invested in solutions, £280 should be generated in benefits.

The benefits are estimated to be:

- Local authorities saving £26.4bn (49%) through reduced use of homeless services of housing and support;
- Improved wellbeing of £14.6bn (27%) by people securing secure housing;
- Increased economic output of £6.5bn (12%) by people entering employment;

---

[114] Report 'Everybody in: How to end homelessness in Great Britain', Crisis, 2018.

- The Exchequer saving £6.4bn (12%) through reduced use of public services such as NHS and criminal justice system services.

The Crisis report referred to nearly 246,000 households needing support in 2018. If we apply a ratio of 1.5 people to a household, as considered earlier in this book, this gives rise to 369,000 homeless people.

If we break the figures down so that they relate to one HYP, the individual costs are £2,752 and the benefits are £7,363 per person per year between 2018 and 2027, and benefits. If you applied these figures to a HYP population of say 200,000 out of the total UK homeless population of 369,000, the discounted costs are £550 million and benefits of £1.47 billion a year. Clearly, more work would be required on these numbers to bring them up to date and relate them to a youth homeless population. However, for the purpose of seeking to consider the resources required, we will use these numbers as a starting position.

Financial resources

We have seen the state of the UK's finances with a huge rising debt and a continuing deficit, together with calls from various departments for more funds. However, we are fortunate in having 136 billionaires listed in the *Sunday Times Magazine* Rich List 2018 – the top 100 had assets valued at £430.7 billion.

While many billionaires have their assets in non-liquid form, such as businesses or property, 10 billionaires have pledged to give away £19.6 billion (at least half their wealth) to charity. Many are charitably minded but may fully support a wide range of other charitable causes and so may not be able or willing to support youth homeless charities.

The top 100 charities reached £9.5 billion in 2015, with Cancer Research UK top of the list, raising £446.5m. However, they then saw the longest fall in voluntary income for 20 years. Their combined income in Quarter 1 2017 was £3.1 billion.[115]

UK and US fundraising

When comparing the UK and US charity sectors, the UK remains one of the most charitable countries in the world, with 79% of people participating in at least one charitable action in 2014. Compared to £10.6 billion donated, the US donations were $358 billion, with 63% of the population donating to a charitable cause. The US benefits from five times the size of population, with a tax situation that provides a greater incentive to donate, despite Gift Aid and the other benefits of donating to charity in the UK.[116]

Jake Hayman, the chief executive of philanthropic advice service Ten Years' Time, explained that we do not have the same social expectations as the US, where philanthropy is worn as a badge of honour. He asserted that, *"British philanthropists tend to work less hard on their charitable giving. They are generally disconnected from the communities they wish to serve and unable to get beyond a couple of sentences of prompt cards when explaining why they give to any particular work."*[117]

Bill Gates, the founder of Microsoft, has become a role model of billionaire philanthropy. Noah Kirsch reported, on 15th August 2017, for *Forbes*, of the mosquito net initiative by the Bill & Malinda Gates Foundation and his charity's broader effort to combat malaria. This is a good example of a philanthropist taking an active approach to a charitable cause and how he has influenced other philanthropists, such as his friend, Warren Buffett.

---

[115] Article 'Top 100 charities see longest fall in voluntary income for 20 years', Rob Preston, 31st January 2018, Civil Society.
[116] Article 'The USA and UK charity sectors compared', Simon Barnes, Alliance Publishing Services, 15th December 2015.
[117] Article 'The Transatlantic giving gap: rich Britons outdone by charitable Americans', Robert Neate, *The Guardian*, 24th November 2017.

As Investopedia reported on 16th July 2018, Mr Buffett's contribution to the charity run by Bill Gates has given him a 'seat at the table' of the Bill and Melinda Gates Foundation and he maintains an active involvement in the organisation. He has a strong interest in philanthropy and in solving global health and educational problems. This led him to actively promote the foundation and encourage others to contribute; especially those with high-value estates.

This illustrates a fundraising approach that we can emulate – to find a well-respected, wealthy businessman to back a charitable cause and encourage others from an extensive, wealthy network to do the same.

Based upon the above projections, if we assume a financial budget of £550 million a year between 2018 and 2027 for combating youth homelessness in the UK, I am concerned that nowhere near this target will be reached if we rely upon the government alone, due to the current debt levels and other funding requirements.

Charity competition

If we look at the money currently being raised by UK charities, the position also looks comparatively weak. In terms of perception, the 2018 YouGov Charity Index showed brands with the highest average index score in the year to 30th June 2018. The Index score was a measure of overall brand health, calculated by taking the average from impression, quality, value, satisfaction, recommend and reputation.

No homeless charities featured in the top 10. In terms of fundraising, in 2017/8, Cancer Research was top of the list, at £433 million. Since that time, charities have found it harder to collect donations.

By getting a wealthy entrepreneur to get behind the cause, we have a chance of making a significant difference. A sound plan can then be constructed, taking account of the financial resources required and the development of high-quality key and support workers to provide the services needed. It will require liaison with homeless charities, local authorities, benefits departments and government about how best to satisfy the housing need.

The scale of the problem

If a plan were to be formulated, based upon a HYP population of 200,000, over what timetable could it be implemented and what infrastructure would be required? Is this target too ambitious and should the action plan run over a longer period? This should become apparent as a plan is developed.

Accommodation

The Westminster Government has set a housebuilding target of 300,000 homes a year for England by the end of the current fixed term parliament to 5th May 2022, but has fallen behind its target, while England needs 3 million new social homes by 2040.[118]

Emergency accommodation should only ever be a temporary solution – people instead need greater entitlement to a home, giving them the best chance of being healthy, having a job and feeling part of society.

To achieve this aim, there needs to be enough housing that homeless people can afford. Based on the earlier projection of around 369,000 homeless people, it was estimated that 100,500 homes a year need to be built over the next 15 years.

There is no 'one size fits all' solution and many HYP are housed in different forms of temporary accommodation. There are also different levels of support needed. It is possible that individuals

---

[118] Article 'England needs 3m new social homes by 2040 says cross-party report', Robert Booth, *The Guardian*, 8th January 2019.

with low support needs could continue in some form of temporary accommodation, if no permanent housing is available, and until permanent housing is ready, if the quality of support is appropriate to move them on to an independent life within a reasonably short timescale.

As many as possible should be moved to a more permanent home, and many of those with high support needs may need to move out of temporary accommodation now. There also has to be 'move-on' accommodation available.

In some parts of the country, there has been a move towards smaller units. While a home with six HYP is one approach, I have seen a very successful outcome from a home abroad that has 60 beds. The difference is in the caring home environment that has been created and the number of live-in and day workers at the home that can make a positive change to the lives of each and every resident.

If there were to be a mix of very large and specifically designed homes that can house say 50 residents (with an appropriate key and support worker network) together with smaller homes that can accommodate up to 10 residents, and a mix of properties of a smaller size for those with high support needs, then this may require a mix of new builds for the larger properties and renting, or for the other homes to be acquired from the private residential sector.

If, for example, we look at a requirement of housing for 200,000 HYP, this could be achieved by a mix of different sized properties, as illustrated below:

- 200 (5%) in specially designed large properties, each housing 50 residents – 10,000;
- 2,000 (10%) in properties, each housing 10 residents – 20,000;
- 20,000 (50%) in properties, each housing five residents – 100,000;

- 23,333 (35%) in smaller properties, each housing three high needs residents – 70,000.

This would give rise to the need for 45,533 properties housing 200,000 HYP, without taking account of young people in crisis, who will need support in future years.

For the projects to be successful, project managers will be required to take overall responsibility for each initiative, with the roles of the project manager and charity clearly identified, and close liaison will be required.

Homeless charity resources

The plan will only succeed if there are the appropriate personnel resources of a sufficient quality within organisations that have the structure and experience to deliver the services required.

Currently, homeless charity workers are having to take on a very high caseload and there are still a vast number of HYP who are getting little or no help. Many charity workers are having to take on all aspects of a client's needs, whereas a few of the larger charities have in-house staff who specialise in a particular area, (for example, counselling, education or employment).

So as to start to provide an illustration of the kind of money needed, if we wish to provide support in the form of say one key worker to live in a home, and be responsible for, say, five HYP while also providing support at the day centre to another five HYP who are in another property but have low support needs, each key worker could handle 10 HYP.

A line manager could oversee five key workers and support workers whom, during the day, act for 50 HYP that have various support needs, so that the support worker will only be advising on one area of specialisation.

If we are to tackle the HYP population of 200,000 that we have identified, this will need significant further recruitment. However, the existing homeless charities are already providing a level of support. If we start by recruiting personnel to support 100,000 HYP, leaving the other 100,000 to be covered by the existing teams within the homeless charities, this would require the recruitment of:

- 10,000 key workers at an average salary of £25,000, costing £250m in total;
- 2,000 line managers at an average salary of £30,000, costing £60m in total;
- 2,000 support staff at an average salary of £25,000, costing £50m in total.

The total estimated cost for the additional 14,000 staff is £360 million a year, plus add-on costs such as employer's NI and pensions. The discounted costs for 200,000 HYP, based on the Crisis/PWC projections, was estimated to be £550 million, and so the above estimated costs of £360 million only leaves £190 million for all other costs. While you would expect a large allocation of the total to staffing, it is likely that the total funding may need to be at a much higher level.

The recruitment policy can be reviewed once the numbers start to fall. The need for 2,000 support workers and 2,000 support staff, together with 10,000 key workers, would require a number of additional large and medium-sized charities.

It may be that the existing HYP charities (in particular the larger charities such as St Mungo's and Centrepoint) can expand to take on a larger client base, but it may be necessary to set up additional charities, possibly linked to the existing network.

The previously illustrated home for six residents with a key worker and support needed charitable donations of around £30,000 up-front and £40,000 a year and a high support ratio, with a view to achieving a quicker move into independence. Other models may not need the same level of support, while some may cost more, if the support needs are very high.

Other issues

When looking at the overall plan, consideration needs to be given to the recruitment policy to attract the staff needed and whether specific courses need to be created at colleges and university. The Crisis report has covered early intervention policies and initiatives, and schools and communities should be involved so as to identify young people in crisis at an early stage.

The poor perception of homeless people should be considered further with a plan to overcome this issue and promote the positive outcomes of action taken to encourage greater participation.

The way forward

These projections are no more than a brief first attempt at trying to identify the scale of the problem and the resources needed to tackle youth homelessness. The numbers need a proper examination by a team of experts who can create a much more meaningful assessment and bring any projections up to date. It then needs to be worked up into a financial plan that can assess the money and people needed and how the targets set will be achieved.

Normally, the job is left to the government to come up with a plan to tackle social issues, but although there may be many talented people in the civil service and at ministerial level, we often fall short of achieving the goals that are set. This may be partly because there is not enough honesty about the scale of the problem, how it is to be tackled and what can be achieved.

I feel privileged to live in a wonderful country that treasures free speech and there are many characteristics that make our country great, but I do feel that sometimes we make progress in spite of ourselves.

One day, someone will write a book (or comedy) about how we went about the Brexit process that has dominated the news headlines while serious social issues have been relegated in importance. Whether you were a Remainer or Leaver, we pressed the button to leave the EU on 29st March 2019, without having worked through the detail. For example, at what point did someone consider how were we going to square the circle of the Irish border question?

If we are to tackle youth homelessness seriously, we need a well-constructed plan that carefully considers all the problems that must be overcome and sets out how that will be achieved.

Many people from various backgrounds enter politics to make a difference. They are often dedicated people who help their constituents on local matters and are devoted to making our lives better. Listening to parliamentary debates, I am often impressed by the quality of the speakers, from a purely intellectual viewpoint. Like eloquent barristers, they can put on a great show but, too often, politics seems to get in the way of achievement. It is sad that the many Oxbridge graduates, the very cream of our education system, leave university and enter politics, but fail to maximise their talent from the public's perspective.

The great achievers are often businessmen, free of the shackles of political correctness. However, these entrepreneurs are not normally in business to create social justice but rather to make money. So we somehow need both parties working together to create a credible plan that can be actioned, monitored and communicated to the public while other, smaller initiatives are put in place.

16

CONCLUSION

Introduction

A great deal of work is needed to permanently reduce youth homelessness but first we need to consider the different areas that require improvement, think through the deficiencies in the system and consider what to change to leave a much-improved legacy for the future. Only then can we see how best to play to our strengths, minimise our weaknesses and make the necessary changes to achieve the goals of the plan.

I do believe that, like the Finnish experience, we must tackle homelessness both nationally and within each community and communicate the outcomes to the public. It is achievable to meet our goals, if we have the moral capacity to do so and the will to take the necessary steps.

Perception

As we have seen, the homelessness charities are currently at a disadvantage, as there is a misperception of youth homelessness that leads to prejudices that exacerbate the problem. The huge 'hidden homeless' population, with many living a chaotic existence in unsuitable temporary accommodation, goes unnoticed and the problems, when identified, are often misunderstood.

Media attention has, understandably, been directed at street homelessness, fake begging and charity failings, but these deflect the more serious, underlying issues. If people received a better understanding of life as a young person in crisis and some of the reasons that have contributed to their plight, there is likely to be more pressure for change and engagement in the solution. Considerable work is needed to better explain the need for support; especially as the number of homeless people in Britain is projected to reach 575,000 by 2041.

Homeless charities need to consider further how and why they are not regarded as highly as other charitable sectors. A campaign should be created to provide periodic updates that reflect progress and the targets to be met. While images portraying street homelessness can be powerful, they ignore the larger, hidden homeless population, and the challenge is to consider how to portray hidden homelessness in a visual form that has the same effect.

Identification

It is difficult to start to reduce numbers of homeless people if we do not know the starting position. Thought is needed as to how best to identify and track these young people. Technology and social media may provide some answers, in this regard. As more HYP are catered for, the position should become clearer. If measures are put in place to better identify the true levels of both core and wider homelessness among the youth, any strategic plan can be updated and the actions required reconsidered. Creativity will be needed to find the best ways to reach HYP and the sources that are to be part of the process, such as schools that often identify family problems at an early time.

The Centrepoint recommendation that central government should sponsor a national, virtual portal giving all young people access to advice and information about homelessness should be adopted. It should be developed as the natural place for HYP to access when in crisis.

Quality and consistency of support

What is needed at this critical time in the life of a HYP is a key worker who wins the young person's trust and has the expertise to provide the support required. We have to ensure that there are sufficiently qualified workers coming through each year and introduce more courses that are specifically designed to attract support workers into the sector. With many seeking long-term employment, this is one sector that is under-resourced and could become an attractive career choice, in the right environment.

There are deficiencies in the provision of support services for homeless people and this needs to be addressed as part of the plan to reduce homelessness; learning from the way that homeless people view service provision. For example, the traditional, some-what institutional approach of seeking to overcome a person's problems without getting to the underlying causes is unproductive, whereas playing to their strengths generally produces better results.

The reduction in drop-in centres and youth clubs needs to be reversed. We have insufficient support providers. It also cannot be stressed enough how important it is to help a young person maximise their educational potential and get into work, as well as prepare them with the necessary life skills (for example cooking, improving interpersonal skills, finance and budgeting, dealing with local authorities etc.) so that they can achieve independence. A mentor, post-independence, can help when things get tough in the real world.

Social issues

A better understanding of the social issues affecting young people is necessary when considering possible action to help young people in crisis. It will also help the public and potential donors gain a better appreciation of what these people face on a daily basis.

It is easy to dismiss someone who has taken drugs or has a record for petty crime without understanding that they may be doing so in an attempt to cope with a chaotic environment. This is not to excuse the situation but to better understand their plight, as many behaviours have developed as a result of some form of past trauma or abuse.

Resident mix

The selection of residents in a home is very important, as ideally you want to see both the individuals and the group prosper, while residents need to buy into the rules of the house so as to avoid disruptive or negative behaviour. In some cases, it may be appropriate to mix people with differing issues, while in other cases, problems can arise if, for example, residents who are still struggling with substance abuse are living with vulnerable young people who have kept away from drug use.

Charity competition

There are a large number of charities competing for funding that may not always be conducive to a close working relationship. In view of the major work required to significantly reduce the HYP population, the inter-charity networks could be reviewed to consider any changes to improve coordinated working. If a national campaign is to be developed, this could bring together the expertise within the various homeless charities as well as other specialist advisers, such as media and public relations consultants.

Accommodation

We need to create homes rather than short-term accommodation, together with a range of services that are tailored to the individual, including preparation for an independent life and move-on accommodation.

Too often, the emphasis has been to get a person off the streets, but the accommodation provided is often not conducive to enable progress to be made and the services are not provided in a manner that is likely to produce the best results and the fastest transition to independence.

There must be a better working relationship with private landlords if they are to be part of the solution due to the current lack of permanent available accommodation. It should be possible to make it attractive for landlords to want to become more involved, if their needs are met.

The available accommodation requires a strategy of its own. The housebuilding targets are not being met and we need pragmatic and realistic solutions. This may involve the following:

- Allowing for the planning of specially constructed properties;
- Better relationships with private landlords to release more housing;
- Converting existing temporary accommodation into permanent housing;
- Converting non-residential property into housing for HYP.

It will require liaison between the funders, local authorities, landlord groups and developers, among others. Housing targets have consistently fallen short and it is important that, in future, they are realistic and fully funded, with the sources of land and buildings identified, together with a creative approach to converting old-style property stock into usable space.

Homeless charities

We have many great charities with dedicated staff, experienced in helping young people in crisis and with a real understanding of the issues they face and how to help them. However, they are under-resourced to handle the current homeless population. The charities also struggle to collect enough money each year to fund their ongoing work without taking on more clients. The resourcing of people and money must be built into a plan for the future.

The homeless charities that have developed successful models can help smaller, regional homeless charities plan their way forward.

Communities

Community initiatives can be very powerful, drawing in providers, donors, and the general public into initiatives that can make a real difference to the lives of young people in crisis. Single faith, as well as inter-faith, projects also help to bind communities and break down barriers.

The state

The state clearly has a responsibility to bring down homeless numbers. At the same time, an assessment of its financial capability must take into account its liabilities and ability to commit funds.

What is required is an honest assessment of the current level of funding that can be committed to homeless reduction, taking account of all the other demands from the various governmental departments. Just as when setting up a home, you ideally want long-term donors to commit to a funding level for a period of time to provide for a sustainable project, you want the state to start with a level of funding that can be assured over a pre-determined time period.

If the state is able to encourage greater wealth creation from the business community, resulting in additional funds for the Treasury, all the better. On the other hand, we live in uncertain times, and when going to print, it is unclear how the current trade war between the US and China will affect the global economy, just as it is unclear how our future relationship with the EU will affect the UK economy.

The move towards Housing First has been slower in the UK than in some countries and this needs to be addressed as part of a wider, integrated and comprehensive strategic approach.

Private sector partners

One of the key elements to creating the environment for homeless reduction is to create a successful, targeted approach to encourage wealthy benefactors to lead initiatives as part of a coordinated approach, working with the state, homeless charities, local authorities, landlords and other relevant partners. This is not to ignore some of the great work already in place, but the scale of the problem does now warrant a fresh look at how we can engage more people in the process.

The ultra-high net worth have the ability to make a huge difference, but I suspect that they will be more encouraged to be part of the solution if they have some form of control over the process: it is their money and they will want to see that it is well spent. Success from one project can have a positive knock-on effect. As one entrepreneur is able to illustrate the outcomes achieved, others are likely to follow.

This point was well illustrated by Theresa Lloyd, the founder director of Philanthropy UK and author of 'Why Rich People Give', who commented, *"The days when wealthy donors just signed cheques are gone; they see themselves as engaged partners. A long-term strategy is essential; getting to know donors and their motivations, explaining the difference donations make to the beneficiaries about whom they care, involving them in projects, being honest about successes and failures, and thanking them. Too many charities do not invest in relationship building, priding themselves instead on how little they spend on fundraising rather than the net sum they raise. People do not just give; they give to a cause that inspires them, and until more charities change their approach we will not have the step change in philanthropic investment in society that we all seek.*"[119]

It cannot be left to the ultra-high net worth alone. The case study showed that a commitment of around £40,000 a year can enable a home to be set up to take six young people in crisis away from homelessness. With Gift Aid tax relief, that cost can come down to around £24,000, or £4,000 per homeless person. Some people may be able to commit to £4,000 a year while for many this will be too high. However, with a group approach, this target can be more easily reached.

We have also seen the other ways in which the public can continue to support homeless reduction, from hosting a young person through the Nightstop scheme, to volunteering, mentoring, and many other different methods.

Priorities

The HYP population includes a wide range of people with different needs and severity of issues to be tackled. While it is important to accommodate these people into permanent homes using the Housing First approach, it is also possible, at the same time, to carefully select the residents and allocate them in a way that is most likely to produce positive outcomes.

The street homeless are the most obvious group at risk, but the hidden homeless are much larger in number. The hostels sector will be very happy to see HYP moving into permanent homes and so freeing up beds. In time, as the homeless in hostels reduce in number, hostels can be converted as part of the process of increasing the number of permanent homes available.

---

[119] Letter to *The Times*, Theresa Lloyd, founder director of Philanthropy UK and author of 'Why Rich People Give', 30th October 2019.

It should also be possible to identify HYP in winter shelters or B&Bs with the right procedures in place to record residents. The most difficult group to identify may be those sofa surfing, and attention is needed to find creative ways of reaching out to the people who may know of those in crisis.

It should be possible to launch homes now and take in those whom the homeless charities identify as needing permanent accommodation while a longer-term plan is put in place to free up the properties that can provide the balance of accommodation required.

A comprehensive plan for the UK

Too often, important issues have been addressed on a superficial basis without including an assessment of the key matters that require attention, along with the detail that shows how the targets are to be achieved. To address a significant reduction in youth homelessness, we need a long-term plan that is both ambitious and achievable, with checks on actual progress on a regular basis and independent progress reports published.

While we find ways to create additional homes and support for the HYP population, we need to consider the wider picture. What comes across, from the experience of international research and from my understanding of the current issues relating to youth homelessness, is the need for a fully integrated UK plan that considers the way in which Housing First should be adopted for homeless people with different support needs.

This comprehensive strategic plan is required to set out the roles for all relevant parties in helping to reduce homelessness, including the government, homeless charities, specialist service providers, local authorities, benefit departments, the state, educational establishments, employment advisers, the private sector, potential funders, private landlords and developers, communities and neighbourhoods. It also needs to ensure that there is a joined-up approach to the process; especially with so many parties involved.

One person with the vision and passion can make a major impact. The plan could be created under the auspices of the people who will be providing the funding, with input and support from all other relevant parties.

A leader needs to bring together a team of key players in the community covering the political establishment, business, religious leaders, respected individuals in the community and leaders of volunteer organisations and unite them with a common vision and achievable goals. It needs a bold approach with the strength to overcome resistance and obstacles.

Where does the money come from?

This is perhaps the most difficult area. If we accept that the government's debt levels and requests for funding from various departments will have an adverse impact on its ability to provide all the money needed to significantly reduce youth homelessness, we need to identify a practical way forward. However, it would also be unreasonable to expect the funding to only come from the private sector, especially as it is the state that will benefit from taking homeless people off its books.

The PWC report for Crisis projected that between 2018 and 2041, for every £100 invested in the solution, £280 should be generated in benefits to the state.

One approach is to have an agreed funding partnership; for example, for every £1 million raised by the private sector, the state must contribute at an agreed level.

Alternatively, the funding could come from the private sector, but with payback from the state to the private sector as each homeless person moves to independence. In this way, the private sector is effectively lending the money needed, which will be returned over time as the homeless numbers fall permanently and the state's costs are reduced, thereby allowing it to repay its debt to the private sector.

The impact that can be achieved

If we are going to seriously reduce youth homelessness in the UK, we need to be in it together. We have seen the reasons for youth homelessness and how many young people's lives have been adversely affected, often by circumstances outside their control. They desperately seek help at this critical time in their lives – not a handout, but support for a short period of time.

I am hopeful that the issues identified can be taken forward into a well-developed and implemented plan so as to create a real change in our society. Positive outcomes should have a galvanising effect of encouraging more people to become involved in the process in whichever way they can, helping young people move to a fully independent life and become valuable members of society.

All forms of homelessness are shocking, but youth homelessness is particularly unacceptable. A young person in crisis needs urgent support, as the effects of homelessness can very quickly lead to more far-reaching and permanent issues. The tragedy is that the likely downward spiral can often be avoided if the right form of support is available at the outset.

We are fortunate to live in a first world country, but how can we allow youth homelessness to exist in such large numbers? Yes, there are many worthy causes, but we can significantly and permanently reduce youth homeless numbers if we can forge a well-constructed partnership between the state and the private sector. There is a role for everyone who wishes to be part of the solution. With homeless numbers rising, we cannot wait for others to take the initiative.

ACKNOWLEDGEMENTS

I would like to record my appreciation for those who have helped in the production of this book as well as the many people who are committed to helping young people in crisis.

My wife, Beverley, has been a wonderful source of encouragement as well as carrying out the laborious task of proof reading. I have also had help with various aspects of the book from Susan Minsky and Dean Harris.

I am grateful to Becky Banning, Tamsin Rush and the other members of the team at the publisher, Grosvenor House, for their professionalism and support.

As you will have seen from the references, I have been able to utilise the extensive research material from homeless charities such as Crisis, Centrepoint and Shelter. There are also many journalists and presenters in the media who continue to raise awareness of the plight of youth homelessness as well as general poverty in the UK.

Private charities and corporate foundations have also been a great support in providing funding for initiatives to reduce youth homelessness.

I have seen at first hand the great work carried out by dedicated staff at the numerous UK and overseas homeless charities in the delivery of services to young people in crisis. Often they are working under great pressure brought about by the increase in homeless people.

I have also met many people working in local authorities and government who wish to make a difference to the lives of others. Greater liaison at local and national level from all these parties will be needed if real progress is to be made in reducing youth homelessness over the next decade.